Forming
Christian Habits
in Post-Christendom

Forming
Christian Habits
in Post-Christendom

The legacy of Alan and Eleanor Kreider
Edited by James R. Krabill and Stuart Murray

 **Herald Press**
Copublished with Institute of Mennonite Studies

Library of Congress Cataloging-in-Publication Data
Forming Christian habits in post-Christendom : the legacy of Alan and
Eleanor Kreider / edited by James R. Krabill and Stuart Murray.
   p. cm.
Includes bibliographical references.
ISBN 978-0-8361-9602-3 (pbk. : alk. paper)
   1. Anabaptists—Missions. 2. Missions—Theory. 3.
Anabaptists—Doctrines.. 4. Christianity and culture. 5. Kreider, Alan,
1941- 6. Kreider, Eleanor, 1935- I. Krabill, James R. II. Murray, Stuart,
1956-
BV2498.F67 2011
266.0092'2—dc23

                      2011022422

FORMING CHRISTIAN HABITS IN POST-CHRISTENDOM
THE LEGACY OF ALAN AND ELEANOR KREIDER
Copyright © 2011 by Herald Press, Harrisonburg, Va. 22802
Published simultaneously in Canada by Herald Press, Waterloo, Ont.
N2L 6H7.
Copublished with Institute of Mennonite Studies,
Associated Mennonite Biblical Seminary, Elkhart, Ind., 46517
Library of Congress Catalog Card Number: 2011022422
International Standard Book Number: 9780836196023
Printed in the United States of America
Book design by Nekeisha Alexis-Baker

To order or request information, please call 1-800-245-7894,
or visit www.heraldpress.com.

: Contents

I.
It all fits together

1

Alan and Eleanor Kreider
A biography

Andrew Kreider and David Nussbaum

Alan and Eleanor Kreider come from American Mennonite families
whose roots extend for centuries into Switzerland and Alsace.

The early years
Alan's story. Alan was born in Goshen, Indiana, on November 8,
1941. Alan's father, Carl, was academic dean of Goshen College and
professor of economics. His mother, Evelyn, was a gracious host
to countless campus visitors. Carl, a gifted administrator, was a
steady, careful academic with a heart to help students in need, a
trait especially evident in the years after World War II in the care
he gave to "mature" students struggling to enter college after years
spent in alternative service as conscientious objectors.

If Alan got his academic gift from his father, his fire in the
belly comes from his mother. Evelyn Kreider faithfully discharged
her duties as a dean's wife, but she has really come into her own in
retirement years, engaging in passionate advocacy work in areas
of justice, peace, and hunger. When Alan becomes exercised as a
speaker, it is his mother's voice that one hears.

From 1952 to 1956 the Kreider family lived in Tokyo, where
Carl was the first dean of International Christian University, a
school founded by Japanese and American Protestants as a way of
repenting for Christian complicity in the horrors of World War II.
Alan attended military and international schools, and was a class-

mate of children from army, diplomatic, and business families. These were formative but difficult years.

Alan attended Goshen College from 1958 to 1962. There he found teachers who nurtured his twin loves of history and music. Mary Oyer attracted him toward musicology. But it was Mary's brother, John Oyer, who eventually won Alan over to the study of history. After graduation from Goshen College in 1962, Alan proceeded directly to graduate school at Princeton University. He had received a lucrative four-year Danforth Fellowship, and his intent was to study the Radical Reformation in German-speaking Europe. But his plans were dashed in his first year at Princeton when he discovered that the professor with whom he intended to study was mortally ill. The Princeton history department tried to persuade him to study the English Reformation instead. Not easily swayed, Alan took a year off to study at Heidelberg University, intending to delve more deeply into the German Reformation.

An invitation to the United Kingdom changed his course. In the spring of 1964, Mary Oyer, who was in Edinburgh studying with musicologist and hymnologist Eric Routley, invited Alan to visit her. He met her in Scotland and traveled with her to visit many churches and cathedrals in England. To his surprise, Alan felt strangely at home in England and sensed that he was being drawn to study English history. Alan decided to return to the United States to do doctoral studies at Harvard University in the English Reformation.

Eleanor's story. Eleanor was born on November 16, 1935. Her parents, J. D. (Joseph) and Minnie Graber, were Mennonite missionaries, based in Dhamtari, in north-central India. Her earliest memories are of India—the landscape, the people, and the English boarding school in Darjeeling from which she twice attempted to escape. During the Second World War, in 1942, the Graber family returned to the United States. After a year in Princeton, during which her father studied at Princeton Theological Seminary, Eleanor and her family moved to northern Indiana, first to the small city of Goshen, and then in 1944 to neighboring Elkhart, where J. D. was general secretary of Mennonite Board of Missions (MBM).

Eleanor's parents were both excellent public speakers. J. D. was the dynamic, engaging preacher whose sermons inspired a generation of postwar Mennonites with a vision of mission that was both global and local. "For every church a mission outpost" was his slogan, which led to the planting of many churches. As a woman Minnie had to work her sermons into the children's times she was allowed to lead during worship services. "Do what they ask you, but always do more," she would tell Eleanor. Her parents' devotion to church and mission, their public ministry gifts, and their regular hospitality for visitors from around the globe—all these shaped Eleanor as she was growing up. But she possessed one gift that her parents lacked: her ability as a musician. In her teenage years, Eleanor excelled both as a pianist and also as the first woman to lead the a cappella singing at Prairie Street Mennonite Church in Elkhart, Indiana, her home congregation.

College years took Eleanor to Hesston College in Kansas and then back to Goshen College to study music. It was at Goshen that Eleanor met Richard Nase, a music student from Souderton, Pennsylvania. They married on June 28, 1958, and their daughter, Joy Ellen, was born on December 31, 1959. Eleanor began her master of arts degree in piano performance at the University of Michigan in 1957, completing it in the summer of 1962. She taught music at Goshen College.

Tragedy struck twice in the early 1960s. Dick died of acute leukemia on December 24, 1961. Then, unthinkably, Joy contracted another aggressive cancer and died on August 6, 1963. The years of illness and grief shaped Eleanor deeply. At College Mennonite Church, the choir she was conducting grew accustomed to her crying through every piece they sang. Good friends—Bettie Norman, Dorothy McCammon, and Mary Oyer—walked with her through the weeping and then the long months and years that followed. Alan, a student six years her junior, was also a friend in these years. He had known Dick and became Eleanor's conversation partner on college choir tours in which she participated as a faculty member.

Courtship, marriage, and parenthood, 1964–67

In 1964 it was one of Eleanor's close friends, Dorothy McCammon, who decided to play matchmaker. It was time, she told Eleanor, that she go to Europe. Alan was in Heidelberg on his year of European study. She thought the two of them should meet there and spend some time together. Eleanor decided to go—setting off that summer with a friend on a ship from Montreal to Rotterdam. Initially her plan was to go to the United Kingdom, with the goal of meeting Mary Oyer in Scotland. But Eleanor went directly to Heidelberg. To the astonishment of both, Eleanor decided to set out with Alan to Athens, where he was to deliver a car to his parents who were arriving after a year of teaching in Ethiopia. Carl and Evelyn were surprised to be met not only by their oldest son but by Eleanor as well.

Eleanor and Alan were married on June 21, 1965. Their first year was spent in Cambridge, Massachusetts, where Alan—at Harvard—turned his focus to the history of the English Reformation and Eleanor taught piano in Wellesley and worked as a secretary for the conductor of the Harvard Men's Glee Club. During this year they made plans to return to England for research, which generous grants enabled them to do the following year.

From 1966 to 1968 Alan and Eleanor lived in London, while Alan completed his PhD research. In those years their home was the London Mennonite Centre, in Highgate, North London—a residence for international students run by workers from MBM. In that era, accommodation for students of color was hard to find, and the Mennonite center was a significant ministry for a long line of students from around the world. During this stay in London, on December 14, 1967, Eleanor and Alan's son, Andrew, was born at the London Hospital in Whitechapel—making him a proper Cockney.

A decade of navigating between England and Indiana, 1968–79

Between 1968 and 1972 Alan and Eleanor taught on the faculty of Goshen College. Then in 1972 they returned to England, this time with funding from the American Council of Learned Societies, so Alan could complete research needed to publish his PhD dissertation in the prestigious Harvard Historical Monographs series. Significantly, this time around they chose not to return to the Mennonite center but rather to live outside the small Mennonite fold, getting to know a wider variety of English friends and contacts. St Albans became their home, a half-hour train journey from the British Library Reading Room in London, but also far enough away that they were able to start afresh.

In these years they made significant connections, as England began to draw them in. Neighbors in their block of flats who were not Christians, local shopkeepers, an organ teacher for Eleanor, worship with Evangelical Anglicans at St. Paul's Hatfield Road, a first encounter with the Post Green community—all were important in their development. They discovered a warm spirit among Anglican friends, and were impressed at the care they saw in study of the Bible, in liturgy, and in prayer. Alan began to get speaking invitations, and his hearers detected something distinctive in his Anabaptist perspectives. After one speech, he recalls thinking, "I may be the first Mennonite to have the chance to speak in England since 1575." Even as Alan was completing his research in preparation for their return to the United States, they found their roots sinking more deeply in the United Kingdom.

This affinity for the United Kingdom did not go unnoticed. In 1973 Wilbert Shenk, then overseas director of MBM, invited the Kreiders to visit him in Aberdeen, where he was on study leave. He proposed that they remain in the UK, and that they return as missionaries under MBM to lead the ministry of the London Mennonite Centre. Alan would carry the official title of warden, but Eleanor and Alan would work together to explore the possibilities of mission in a culture that Shenk believed was rapidly taking on the characteristics of post-Christendom.

They did not have formal mission training, nor did they have theological degrees. Yet Shenk considered them to be the right people at the right time. Among the Mennonite mission workers in Europe, Alan and Eleanor found themselves to be elder figures.

The previous generation of mission workers had mostly left the scene, and the Kreiders were now in place with a dynamic group of mission colleagues—in several countries—who were ten or more years younger than they.

The sense of being untrained for their work was to become a recurring theme, especially for Alan. This Harvard-educated academic often felt out of his depth in fields of other people's expertise. In his speaking and writing in recent years, Alan has reflected on the way these experiences of dis-ease and relative powerlessness formed him. As God placed him in situations where he could not rely on his own strength and academic preparation, he needed to learn to "lean on the Lord" as he studied informally—the Church of Scotland Bible teacher Jim Punton was an important influence—and as he trained himself.

For the first five years of their work in London, Alan remained on the faculty of Goshen College, teaching quarter-time in the United States and also for American student groups who visited London. His courses on the English Reformation and on "Comparative Revolutions" were popular with students. But by the end of the 1970s it was becoming clear that ministry in London was where the Kreiders' heart was. In the summer of 1979, Alan finally formally severed ties with Goshen, moving to full-time work with MBM, as he and Eleanor were committing themselves to a long-term, full-time presence in England.

Eleanor and Alan's decision to leave Goshen and become mission workers caused consternation for some people. His uncle and father, both deeply involved at Goshen College, struggled to reconcile themselves to Alan's departure, which seemed to them a repudiation of his high-powered academic training. Eleanor's parents were more understanding, having made a similarly countercultural move in going to India in the 1920s.

In the winter and spring of 1979, the Kreiders were in Goshen. While Alan taught at Goshen College, Eleanor pursued theological studies at two nearby institutions, Associated Mennonite Biblical Seminary and the University of Notre Dame, with a particular focus on the life and worship of the early church. These studies

were to launch her into a decade of liturgical studies on her return
to England.

Putting down roots at the London Mennonite Centre, 1979–91

Preaching. When they arrived at the London Mennonite Centre,
the Kreiders joined themselves to the London Mennonite Fellowship, a small chaplaincy ministry which met in the center's chapel.
With the encouragement of Stephen Longley, one of the students in
the house, this ministry was reshaped into a worshiping congregation. Alan became the primary preacher, reading long and extensively footnoted sermons from the wooden table in the middle of
the front-room chapel. This was the beginning of his formation as
a preacher.

Ordination. In 1975 Alan was ordained for ministry by a gathering of distinguished visiting Mennonite leaders, including John
Howard Yoder, Albert Meyer, and J. D. Graber. At the same service,
José Gallardo was ordained for ministry in Spain. Significantly, and
as a mark of the times, Eleanor was not considered for ordination.
By her account, it did not occur to her to ask for this step. The title
"reverend" was not one that Alan used in a country in which titles
and class play such a significant role in opening doors and finding
one's place. Indeed, to refer to Alan as having been ordained, unlike
Eleanor, has a paradoxical element, as he would sometimes argue
that one implication of the priesthood of all believers is the abolition
of the laity: all Christians are "ordained."

In any case, to be American in the United Kingdom is to be an
outsider—tolerated for the most part, looked down on and envied at
the same time, but above all not "one of us." To be an academic "doc-
tor" made Alan more acceptable in academic and some religious settings, when his American accent and upbringing could be a liability.

Translation and publishing. During these years, in his spare
time Alan worked on a translation from French of the seminal work
by Jean-Michel Hornus on the early church and warfare: *It Is Not
Lawful for Me to Fight* (1980). And in 1979 Alan finally completed
his book on the English Reformation: *English Chantries: The Road*

to Dissolution. This book was well received by academics in the field and continues to be used today. But Alan was aware that his identity as an academic historian was taking a backseat to his church work.

Speaking and debating. The 1980s saw a new and more public phase in Alan and Eleanor's ministry in England. Increasingly Alan was invited to speak at churches and public gatherings, especially on Christian discipleship and attitudes to war—particularly as the Falklands War of 1982 reignited debates about "just" war—and sometimes about peace—around the United Kingdom. Prominent evangelical Anglican leader John Stott invited Alan to be part of conversations and debates in which various approaches to nuclear armaments were presented. The highest profile event took place in 1983 at All Souls' Church, Langham Place, in central London. There Alan debated the arms race with the former chief of the defence staff, marshal of the Royal Air Force, Sir Neil Cameron. Eleanor and Alan's influence in the United Kingdom extended across the Christian spectrum, but was perhaps particularly significant and influential in the broadly evangelical sections and among those focused on the more radical social, political, and economic implications of the gospel.

Peace advocacy. The ministry of the London Mennonite Centre developed during the 1980s. With the decline in need for international student housing, the student ministry came to a close. As students moved out of the center, church members moved in to take their place, forming a large community household which lived, ate, and worshiped together. Many of them—not least Alan and Eleanor—were active in the peace movement of the 1980s, debating issues of war and peace, and worshiping outside military bases, and on at least one occasion outside the US embassy in London.

Generating and offering resources. Meanwhile, the center began to develop as a resource center in the Anabaptist tradition. Its library and its Metanoia Book Service were useful to pastors, scholars, church planters, and peace activists. Its Cross-Currents weekends, on themes including "Social Holiness," "Power or Powertrip," "Women and Men Together," and "Worship in the World," attracted people who were hunting for alternative ways to follow

Jesus. These events also provided opportunities for Eleanor and Alan to demonstrate their remarkable practice of speaking alternately from a single script, and to design and present material with other members of the church and supporters of the center, such as David Nussbaum, around the United Kingdom and Ireland.

Themes that recur in their work in the 1980s were integrative: grace and peace, shalom, and social holiness. These were captured in Alan's book of 1986, *Journey towards Holiness*, in which he presented his case for a biblical vision of social holiness that fitted together justice, peace, and joy in the Holy Spirit (Rom. 14:17). The election of a Conservative government with Margaret Thatcher as prime minister in 1979 made much of this material even more pertinent, as the United Kingdom faced a prolonged period of social and economic disruption and eventual recovery.

Congregational leadership. The 1980s also saw the ongoing transformation of the London Mennonite Fellowship. The church attracted new members from across London, with the London Mennonite Centre building functioning as the fellowship's base and the home of the intentional community, as well as the center's own operational premises. Combining all three functions in the one building led to difficulties at times, and in due course the fellowship moved its base out of the center. After trying several different locations, it eventually settled in a community center a few miles away in north London, becoming the Wood Green Mennonite Church. Alan and Eleanor continued to be involved as elders in the shared leadership of the group, helping the young church work through questions of decision making and governance. But by the late 1980s they stepped down from leadership positions as more indigenous leaders joined the eldership team.

Itinerant ministry throughout the United Kingdom and beyond, 1991–2000

The end of the 1980s brought a shift in focus: the time to leave London was approaching. Andrew had departed for college in 1987. Now MBM told Eleanor and Alan that for the ministry of the Mennonite center to thrive, they needed to move on and leave the work to others. Another development in the 1980s demonstrated that wider horizons would also be beneficial to them: the formation of the Radical Reformation Study Group (RRSG) was evidence of a growing interest in Anabaptist approaches to theology and discipleship, building on the Kreiders' decision to study and popularize the early church. The RRSG had gathered professional and amateur theologians, from London and further afield, to study and discuss Anabaptist theology and practice. Reflecting Alan's interest in historical rootedness, the group spent a fair proportion of its time working through Walter Klaassen's *Anabaptism in Outline* (1981), which helped build relationships and understanding as well as providing substance to their thinking. From this study group later emerged the Anabaptist Network, a hub for individuals, communities, and organizations with an interest in—and some sense of connection to—Anabaptism.[1]

In 1991, from the stability of a London base, Alan and Eleanor launched out into a more itinerant ministry. This change led them to accept invitations to speak beyond the United Kingdom: a highlight was preaching to thousands of people gathered at Assembly 13 of the Mennonite World Conference in Calcutta, India. Closer home they devoted themselves to nurturing a network of people across the United Kingdom who were interested in Anabaptist theology, which fostered the development of the Anabaptist Network.

During the 1990s Eleanor and Alan lived in two cities. Their first move, in 1991, was north to Manchester, to become theologians in residence at Northern Baptist College. Alan also taught a course in the life and worship of the early church at the University of Manchester. After four years, in 1995, they moved again, this time to Oxford, where Alan became a fellow of Regent's Park College and the first director of the college's Centre for the Study of Christianity and Culture, and Eleanor was a tutor in worship and liturgy. These years drew both Alan and Eleanor back into the academic world—teaching in universities, supervising students, collaborating with graduate fellows, developing significant series of

---

[1] See www.anabaptistnetwork.com.

lectures in Oxford, writing and editing books. It was in her Oxford office that Eleanor wrote *Communion Shapes Character* (1997).

In both Manchester and Oxford the Kreiders were members of Baptist congregations. Their wider ecumenical connections continued, as they visited and spoke to Christian groups from Catholic to Pentecostal; especially they were nurtured by their times in monastic communities, beginning with the Communauté de Grandchamp, an order of sisters in the Swiss Reformed Church who live by the Rule of Taizé. As a balance to the academic world, in Oxford they were committed participants in "Group," a table fellowship that met weekly, and they found places to serve people in poverty.

While at Oxford, they convened an "accountability group" of three respected friends, Stuart Murray, Anne-Wilkinson Hayes, and David Nussbaum. This group, which became especially important to Eleanor and Alan, met with them three times a year, to reflect on the shape of their work and to give counsel on priorities and decisions. In their leadership role in the Anabaptist Network, the Kreiders traveled extensively, nurturing an ever-growing network of study groups, and leading a trip to the Netherlands to see some of the early Mennonite and Anabaptist sites. During this time Alan collaborated with Stuart Murray to edit *Coming Home* (2000), in which more than sixty contemporary Anabaptists in Britain and Ireland tell their stories. This collection indicates the extent of Anabaptism's influence in the United Kingdom by that time.

Encouraging this new network was rewarding and fruitful work, and by the end of the decade the Kreiders found that the network was no longer depending on them. Gifted young leaders had emerged who could carry the work forward and give it greater breadth and renewed intellectual vigor. So the Anabaptist Network officially released them, and after more than twenty-five years of work in the United Kingdom, they prepared for their reentry into the United States.

Back to the United States as mission educators, professors, and grandparents, 2000–

In 2000 Alan and Eleanor moved back to the United States, settling in Elkhart, Indiana. At first they served as itinerant "mission educators" for MBM, traveling several times to the Orient and Australasia, and making yearly return visits to the United Kingdom to travel and teach—not least for "Workshop," the Anabaptist-flavored leadership and discipleship training program with which they had worked. By 2004, this transitional time had run its course. They had left the United Kingdom emotionally as well as physically, and they were finally becoming settled in their new setting. In 2004 Alan joined the faculty of Associated Mennonite Biblical Seminary in Elkhart, teaching courses in church history and mission. Occasionally he and Eleanor traveled to churches for weekend speaking engagements.

But this new phase marked more of a move toward retirement. Alan took pleasure in being back in the classroom, and after all the intervening years, in being a historian again. Eleanor gave significant time to involvement in her local church—Prairie Street Mennonite Church. And both enjoyed their important role as grandparents. In 2009 Alan officially retired from the seminary, opening the door to more time for research and writing. That same year Eleanor and Alan completed a book, *Worship and Mission after Christendom*, which sums up their lives and concerns. In November 2010, at the request of Prairie Street Mennonite Church, Eleanor was ordained for her ongoing ministry across the Mennonite church.

A lifetime of working as a team

Throughout their lives Alan and Eleanor have worked as a team. Alan was appointed warden of the London Mennonite Centre; Eleanor was his wife. But as the years went by, it became evident that Eleanor was a gifted speaker and writer in her own right. While other husband-wife teams were occasionally speakers at events, Eleanor and Alan proved to have a particular gift in communication.

For many people who heard them speak, the most lasting impact was not the content of their presentation but the way they work as a team. Using a single script, they would finish each other's sentences, moving easily from one point to the next, engaging their listeners. Eleanor's easy smile and gentler pace made a good foil to Alan's passion and excitability. On his own, Alan's intensity could sometimes overwhelm an audience. Eleanor would stand on his foot or kick his leg as a reminder to ease up. Their speaking style was something of a high-wire act. At any point, either could wander from the script, following a spontaneous tangent. The tangent over, the other person would rein things in by repeating the last phrase and then moving back on track.

In preparing their speeches, the two would study together, reading commentaries aloud and brainstorming about what they wanted to say. Eleanor is the popularizer, concerned more to communicate important ideas by means of visual images, and not getting lost in details. Alan is the academic, concerned for consecutive argument and getting the details right (including his beloved footnotes). Together they made a good combination—but only after many long hours of discussion. In the end, when they had talked over what they want to say, Alan would go and write a draft text, which Eleanor would revise. As the years went by, they became comfortable doing many presentations with less preparation. They wouldn't know who was going to say the first words, or who would say which parts of the talk. They followed each other's lead, and neither dominated. The intensive preparation meant that they were not able to give as many presentations as they could have if they had each worked alone—but the work they did together had a significant impact, not only in its content but also as an icon of biblical equality.

In the coming phase of their lives, it is likely that Alan and Eleanor will work more independently of each other. Having shared a ministry for so many years, the later chapters of their life's work will be as separate individuals, supporting each other in parallel activities. Eleanor is becoming an active leader in her local congregation, doing more extroverted work. Alan, by contrast, is moving toward scholarly work, coupled with occasional teaching in seminary classrooms. He has at least one more lengthy book left to write—a study of the growth of Christianity in the Roman and Persian empires in the first five centuries. Their life as a couple will continue to manifest values that have been present all along— especially hospitality, with their table at the center as a place of conversation, delicious food, and the discovery of God's presence among those gathered. And Eleanor will continue to begin meals by repeating the phrase, "Happy are those who share a meal in the kingdom of God."

Speaking together
for Alan and Eleanor Kreider
June 10, 2000

Veronica Zundel

not a ball
batted to this point, to that, a click
and click—
no, not that;
not the flash, clash, pierce of swords,
the blade's debate, the thrust, the cutting glance;
not the fisticuffs of raw-boned
blows, or wild
explosions lobbed from safety in dark armor;

more like a plait of two cords woven
this way, that way, a growing rope
with a third cord joining, golden gleaming—from where?—
or weavers casting a shuttle, this side, that
and the weft steadily filling the warp, colors gathering—

no, not that either—a courtly dance then,
bowing, turning, changing and passing a smile:
sometimes a stately gavotte, sometimes a gay
dos-à-dos, a set to the left and right,
a reel, a whirl, and back to the promenade—

or is it a relay, a baton
of wisdom flying past sight from hand to hand?

I think a choir, two voices in harmony—
one rising and then the other, soaring in song:
a sweet duet that transforms to polyphony;
an intimate air for two where all can join in.

Music and worship. When she was a student at Elkhart High School, Eleanor rode her bicycle to the school early in the mornings so that she could practice on the grand piano, giving evidence of what would become a lifelong involvement in music.

International travel. Eleanor and Alan have traveled extensively to converse with Christians from varied countries and cultures. In 1966 they depart the home of Eleanor's parents on Dinehart Avenue in Elkhart (near where they live now) to England where Alan began doctoral research in history.

Community. The London Mennonite Centre community became family to those who lived there, including this 1981 group that comprised people from India, Pakistan, New Zealand, Canada, the United Kingdom, and the United States. Andrew Kreider, son of Alan and Eleanor, is in the center of the back row, Eleanor is in the center of the middle row and Alan is on the left in the front. Below, sometime around 2000, Alan and Eleanor stand in front of their garden flat in the London Mennonite Centre.

Family. Andrew Kreider, son of Eleanor and Alan, was ordained in 1998 for ministry at Prairie Street Mennonite Church, Elkhart, where he served for eleven years.

Currently Alan and Eleanor enjoy close contact with their family in the Elkhart and Goshen area. Below, three generations plus a friend and a pet pose with Alan and Eleanor circa 2005: In front are Joshua Stoltzfus and grandsons Daniel (holding April the dog) and Joseph. Next to Alan is his mother, Evelyn Burkholder Kreider. Katie Fairfield Kreider, Andrew's wife, is holding Eleanor Rose (Rosie), and Andrew is standing at the back.

Witness and activism. Eleanor and Alan participate in public events that give them opportunities to express their faith and commitments. This peace rally in London included friends and members of the Wood Green Mennonite Church.

Baptism and new life. Alan and Eleanor's Elkhart home is graced with a sign, "The Eighth Day," designed for them in Welsh slate by a contributor to this book, Anne Wilkinson-Hayes. The term is an early Christian designation for the first day of the new creation and signifies baptism, resurrection, and the hospitality of God's kingdom.

Working as a team. Eleanor and Alan have a distinctive way of collaborating as they teach and engage their listeners. They share a single outline, spontaneously alternating their voices and perspectives.

Teaching and resource creation. Opportunities continue to open for Alan and Eleanor to share their scholarship widely. A thirteen-year relationship with Youth with a Mission resulted in a DVD project in which Alan recorded six half-hour presentations on the early church. He enlisted the help of Andy Alexis-Baker, a graduate of AMBS, to develop the study questions for the brochure in the DVD box.

Learning from global Christians. Rick Lin (Lin Xing-Dao), a member of the Xi-An Mennonite Church in Taipei, was serving as a deacon in the church at the time that Eleanor and Alan visited Taiwan. Learning from Christians like Mr. Lin in many parts of the world has been a reward of the itinerant ministry that Alan and Eleanor have been doing for the last two decades.

Congregational life. Eleanor Kreider's ordination on November 5, 2010, allowed the Prairie Street Mennonite Church retrospectively to acknowledge her life of ministry. This congregation and the London Mennonite Fellowship (later the Wood Green Mennonite Church) are among the faith communities in which the Kreiders have shared their gifts and received counsel and support.

2

Forming Christian habits in post-Christendom

The missio Dei *approach develops like this. The triune God created the cosmos in love. Genesis 1 portrays God creating the cosmos to be "good," even "very good;" that is to say, God's creation was full of shalom, marked by relationships that were comprehensively, multidimensionally right. God's love was self-emptying and nonviolent. In love, God would not coerce worship or require obedience.*

Humans, however, chose autonomy and disobedience. God had created them, male and female, to be in fellowship with God, to be in right relationship with each other, and to be the stewards of creation. But they chose not to ascribe worth to the God who had created and loved them. The result was painful. Their "Fall" led to brokenness and alienation. This caused anguish to God. God in love has been pained by the marring of his relationship with humans, by the crippling of humans' relationships with each other, and by the blighting of creation that resulted from human disobedience.

God in love is determined to make things right, to counter the Fall and to restore shalom, *and in the fullness of time God will accomplish this. This is God's mission, or as some liberation theologians put it, "God's project."* [1] *As Chris Wright has argued throughout his book, the mission of God is the Bible's "grand narrative."* [2]

---

[1] Jean-Paul Audet, *The Gospel Project* (New York: Paulist Press, 1969).

[2] Christopher Wright, *The Mission of God* (Downers Grove, IL: InterVarsity Press, 2006), 47.

The goals of God's mission are huge. God's mission is to bring God's kingdom, God's redemptive reign. God's mission is creation encompassing. It is to recreate creation, to bring new creation (Isa. 65:17; 66:22; Gal. 6:15). God's mission is to make all things new (Col. 1:20; Rev. 21:5)— humans with "hearts of flesh" in a right relationship to God (Ezek. 36:26), humans reconciled to their bitterest enemies (Is. 19:23–24), and the whole creation restored as a place where justice is at home (2 Pet. 3:13). In all these dimensions—humans with God, humans with other humans, humans with creation—God's project is shalom, an all-comprehending wholeness (Col. 1:20). God's mission is peace . . .

But what means would God use to bring this about? From the beginning of the Bible's metanarrative, God's means was not force; it was not compulsion. God, both before and after the Fall, is self-limiting. God will not coerce worship or force obedience. Instead God's strategy and action are characterized by sending. Sending (missio), *not compelling, is God's* modus operandi:

- *Sending Abram and Sarai to leave security in Mesopotamia to be a blessing for* all the families *of the earth (Gen. 12:1–3).*

- *Sending the people of Israel to be "a royal priesthood and a holy nation" (Exod. 19:6) and a corporate participant in God's mission.*

- *Sending the prophets who state a vision of a servant who will announce and enact the gospel of peace (Isa. 52:7).*[3]

- *Sending, in the fullness of time, Jesus of Nazareth, who as second Adam obediently recapitulates the story of Adam, embodying the vision and making peace by his life, death, and resurrection.*[4]

- *Sending the Holy Spirit on the disciples and the church, empowering them to be corporately sent by the resurrected Jesus.*

---

[3] Willard Swartley, "The Evangel as Gospel of Peace," in *Evangelical, Ecumenical, and Anabaptist Missiologies in Conversation: Essays in Honor of Wilbert R. Shenk*, ed. James R. Krabill, Walter Sawatsky, and Charles van Engen (Maryknoll, NY: Orbis Books, 2006), 69–77.

[4] Eric Osborn, "Love of Enemies and Recapitulation," *Vigiliae Christianae* 54, no. 1 (2000): 12–31.

- *Sending the church to be a light to the nations, to bear witness to Christ and the kingdom, and to be the primary instrument of God's mission.*

- *Sending all Christians to incarnate and enact the way of Jesus in the world: "Peace be with you. As the Father has sent me, so I send you. Receive the Holy Spirit" (John 20:21–22).*

Sending—this is the means of the God of mission. It is the sending—the missio—of God. How risky it all is! How vulnerable the work of a God who entrusts the healing of his broken creation to fallible humans—and who takes flesh that humans can torture and crucify. As Darrell Guder has commented, "It has always been possible for humans to encounter God's Word and work in history and to ignore it, to reject it, to distort it, or to manipulate it for selfish ends . . . God respects the freedom of the creation but mercifully does not treat us the way we treat him." [5] *And through it all, and in untold ways that will transcend it all, God is working to bring his kingdom of reconciliation and joy.* [6]

....

⦂ James R. Krabill and Stuart Murray

The title of this book, *Forming Christian Habits in Post-Christendom*, locates it in a particular historical context. Much of Alan and Eleanor Kreider's ministry has been spent in the emerging post-Christendom culture of England. They now live in a nation that cannot technically experience post-Christendom, if the term implies transition from a formal partnership between church and state. However, the word *Christendom* refers not only to a political arrangement but also to a civilization founded on a supposedly Christian ideology.

---

[5] Darrell Guder, *The Continuing Conversion of the Church* (Grand Rapids, MI: Eerdmans, 2000), 74.

[6] Reprinted from *Worship and Mission after Christendom*, by Alan and Eleanor Kreider. Copyright © 2011 by Herald Press, Scottdale PA 15683. Used by permission.

Christendom is unraveling

In most Western nations, Christendom is unraveling. Fewer people know its foundational story or literature. Congregations and other Christian institutions are becoming marginal, and Christians find themselves constituting one of several religious minorities in a plural society. The center of gravity of the global Christian community is no longer within the boundaries of what was once Christendom but in Africa, Latin America, and parts of Asia. Whether the United States will follow the same trajectory as other Western nations, albeit a generation or two later, or prove to be an exception is debated by sociologists and missiologists.[7]

Many Christian leaders in America, however, are now convinced that their future is some version of post-Christendom and are encouraging young adults to spend time in Europe to learn how to engage with this reality. Alan and Eleanor represent the prescience of an earlier generation of leaders who encouraged them to be long-term missionaries in post-Christendom England. Their experience and writings are a gift to North American churches as well as a resource for Christians in Britain. Drawing deeply on the Anabaptist tradition—which has challenged the Christendom mindset for nearly five centuries—and learning from the pre-Christendom early churches, the Kreiders have consistently presented themes and perspectives that are crucial for post-Christendom Christians.

In the post-Christendom era, *missiology* must precede *ecclesiology*

Missio Dei is a post-Christendom approach to missiology, locating "sending" in the heart of God rather than in ecclesial strategy. In the Christendom era, ecclesiology preceded missiology as the institutional church took center stage and sought to extend its influence in various ways, some less consistent than others with its founding story and values. Post-Christendom requires and enables recovery

---

[7] See, for example, Philip Jenkins, *The Next Christendom: The Coming of Global Christianity* (Oxford: Oxford University Press, 2002); and Peter Berger, Grace Davie, and Effie Fokas, *Religious America, Secular Europe? A Theme and Variations* (Aldershot, England: Ashgate, 2008).

of a more authentic approach to mission, one with a goal more comprehensive and inspiring than just enlarging the influence of the church, and one that adopts attitudes and methods more consistent with the ways Jesus embodied and advanced the mission of God.

But as we pursue a post-Christendom missiology, we must recognize the enduring and frequently maligned legacy of Christendom. As Darrell Guder comments in the passage quoted by the Kreiders above, it is possible for humans to distort God's word and work.

"God's mission" in Christendom was distorted in three principal ways

We will focus here on three examples of distortion that need to be challenged and realigned if we are to move forward more faithfully in the emerging culture of post-Christendom.

The loss of the apostolic function and calling. First, most Christians in the Christendom period had little or no awareness of being sent. In a world in which almost everyone was Christian by dint of being born within the territorial boundaries of a supposedly Christian society, evangelists and evangelism had no relevance. In a society that was ruled by divinely authorized monarchs, there was no need for prophetic witness or campaigns for social justice.

The New Testament ministries particularly associated with movement, pioneering, and being sent—apostles, prophets, and evangelists—were generally regarded as obsolete when the church had achieved an authoritative role within a Christianized society. But the settled and nurturing ministries of pastors and teachers were still required, and these came to dominate perceptions of ministry. Only in persecuted dissident movements, including Anabaptism, did these abandoned forms of ministry reappear from time to time.

Some forms of mission were, of course, still relevant at the boundaries of Christendom. Sometimes dedicated and courageous missionaries, sent out not by local congregations but by papal decree or as members of missionary orders, carried the gospel into distant lands. Sometimes the reach of Christendom was extended by force of arms as soldiers or crusaders, fighting under the sign of the cross, required conversion and imposed the rule of the church on conquered territories. But these expressions of mission were exceptional and disconnected from the worship, community life, and concerns of most local churches.

These distortions need to be recognized and challenged if Christians in post-Christendom societies are to respond effectively to the opportunities and challenges we face. In many congregations, mission is still associated with other people and other places. We need to recover an awareness that all Christians are caught up in the mission of God and are sent—whether locally or globally. We need to rehabilitate the neglected pioneering ministries and integrate these with pastors and teachers into a more holistic and multidimensional approach to Christian ministry. We must train and release apostles and prophets as well as pastors and teachers. And we must reconnect mission and the worshiping community—as the Kreiders have insisted throughout their ministry and in their most recent book, *Worship and Mission after Christendom*.[8]

The loss of risk taking and vulnerability. Second, as Alan and Eleanor say in the above extract, the missio Dei involves vulnerability and risk. The story of the Incarnation illustrates this truth in such an extraordinary way. The birth and early years of Jesus were fraught with insecurities and dangers. The ministry of Jesus provoked great opposition, against which he had no defense that would not compromise his mission; it ended in the apparent defeat of crucifixion. Entrusting the infant church and its continuing participation in the missio Dei to disciples who had abandoned him and had frequently misunderstood his message was an incredibly risky step for Jesus to take. And the story of the spread of the church in the book of Acts is shot through with dangers and difficulties.

After three centuries of marginality, illegality, and sporadic persecution, Christian leaders in the fourth century understandably welcomed the safety and security offered by the emperor Constantine I. Freed from fear and uncertainty, the church could grow

---

[8] See n6 above.

steadily and become established at the heart of the empire. In the Christendom era, there was no longer any risk in being a Christian. On the contrary, it was increasingly risky not to be.[9]

Safety and security appeared to be important gains, but did the church in the Christendom era lose something significant? It may be that another distorting and debilitating aspect of the Christendom legacy is the disjunction of mission and risk taking. Many congregations are instinctively conservative, cautious, and risk averse. The mantra too often seems to be: "Let's not try it in case it doesn't work." A prayer regularly heard in church services today is one thanking God that the congregation is free to meet without fear of opposition—whereas the early Christians (and persecuted Christians through the centuries) rejoiced that they were considered worthy of suffering for the sake of Christ. And what do we make of a major denomination that has an official policy of "risk-free mission"?

Persecution may seem a remote prospect for most Christians in post-Christendom Western societies (although it is a reality for converts from other religions in Western societies), but we are likely to be increasingly vulnerable as our numbers decrease and our social and political influence fades. Perhaps it is time we challenged the safety-first culture in many of our churches—most of which are located in the safer parts of town. Maybe riskier forms of mission will be needed if we are to have an impact on societies that associate the Christian faith with an outdated worldview, a fading culture, and an insurance policy for life beyond death.

The loss of shalom as primary means for carrying out God's mission. Third, the most serious distortion of the missio Dei in the Christendom era was surely the propensity of the church to employ and justify violence for missional ends. If the goal of God's mission, as the Kreiders insist, is all-embracing shalom (including the reconciling of enemies), then those who participate in this mis-

---

[9] See Alan Kreider, *The Change of Conversion and the Origin of Christendom* (Harrisburg, PA: Trinity Press International, 1999); and Stuart Murray, *Post-Christendom: Church and Mission in a Strange New World* (Carlisle, Cumbria, England: Paternoster Press, 2004).

sion cannot use means that so starkly contradict the ends. If God refrains from using force or violence to compel obedience or move forward the missio Dei, those who are sent "to incarnate and enact the way of Jesus in the world" cannot condone violence in the pursuit of any aspect of this mission.

There have always been Christians who knew this and rejected the use of force to achieve missional goals. The Anabaptists and many dissenting communities who were passionately committed to mission recovered marginalized pioneering ministries and were ready to take risks in spite of the severe consequences in order to participate in God's mission. For these communities pacifism was in no way equated with passivism.

But the use of violence—*within* Christendom to suppress dissent and heresy, and *beyond* Christendom to extend the rule of the church—was endemic for many centuries. Sophisticated theological arguments were deployed to justify this violence, and serious attempts were been made to restrain it by imposing conditions, but these were of little comfort to the millions tortured, brutalized, oppressed, and slaughtered in the name of Christ.

Post-Christendom requires a Christian community that wholeheartedly renounces the use of violence and commits itself unreservedly to use only peaceful means in the pursuit of the goal of shalom toward which the mission of God is heading. Many Christians in post-Christendom England seem to be moving in this direction. These encouraging signs may or may not be related to the widespread disquiet about the invasion of Iraq in 2003, but the attitudes of churches and other Christian groups have been surprising since then. Rather than being resistant to the suggestion that violence is unacceptable for those who follow Jesus, many Christians have been receptive to this idea and even seem to struggle to understand why anyone would oppose this view.

This changing reality makes one wonder, in fact, whether the legacy of Christendom and its distortions of the missio Dei may be less powerful than we often imagine. It is not unusual to encounter Christians in many contexts who are unfazed by the prospect of risky missional initiatives, with limited or nonexistent financial and institutional support, and who are willing to invest their lives in pioneering activities that might well not succeed.[10]

Needed: A vision of the missio Dei rooted in the biblical grand narrative

What many of these pioneers—and all of us in post-Christendom—need is a vision of the missio Dei that is rooted in the "grand narrative" of the Bible and expressed in images and language that inspire and sustain courageous missional discipleship. For too long the concepts of shalom and missio Dei have been the preserve of theologians and the tiny minority who read what they write. Only now are they filtering down into the lives and imaginations of many Christians. But when they do, the lights go on, eyes light up, and all kinds of things fall into place.

One of the most significant contributions of Alan and Eleanor Kreider has been their ability to make these foundational concepts of missio Dei and shalom accessible to Christians on the threshold of post-Christendom. They have helped us see how mission and worship, peace and evangelism, hospitality and justice, lifestyle and witness can and in fact *must* be integrated. These diverse aspects all fit together because they are all essential parts of God's comprehensive plan to address the comprehensive brokenness in which we and the world tragically find ourselves.

In the earliest stages of discussion about creating a volume that would celebrate the Kreiders' important contribution to the church's thinking and practice in these matters, the idea emerged of producing a more traditional scholarly piece designed to bring together academics who represent wide-ranging disciplines and who have, in one way or another, been influenced by the Kreiders' writings, life, and ministry.

There was, however, something strangely incongruous about such a plan. Not because the Kreiders have over the years failed to generate serious and prolific scholarly reflection (a quick glance at their extensive bibliography at the end of the present volume will

---

[10] I (Stuart) am privileged to work with some of these in the pioneering church planting agency, Urban Expression (www.urbanexpression.org.uk).

serve as ample demonstration of this fact!), but because they have been equally if not more passionate about "extending the table" and bringing the whole of Christ's body into the conversation.

Not surprisingly, when the Kreiders caught wind of the project underway, their reaction was immediate and their appeal crystal clear: "Please make of any such piece something that builds the church, something rooted in the daily reality of God's people, something that equips and empowers followers of Jesus to live out more faithfully their calling as active participants in God's reconciling mission in the world."

The form and content of the current volume

We as editors have attempted to honor that request. The result is the present volume—a conversation in the form of written reflections grouped around the three primary themes that seem to best capture the message Alan and Eleanor have so faithfully and energetically communicated over the years: *mission, community,* and *worship*.

In each of these three areas, four subthemes develop in more depth various aspects of the primary theme. For *mission,* they are holistic mission, social holiness, pacifism, and Anabaptism; for *community* they are catechesis and baptism, friendship, peace church, the early churches; and for *worship* they are prayer, communion, multivoiced worship, worship and mission). In each of these subchapters, the reader will find a similar sequence of features: a relevant excerpt from one or more of the Kreiders' writings; a substantial essay treating the particular theme being highlighted; and then two shorter reflections on the same topic offered by people involved in a wide range of professions and ministries in places scattered across the globe.

Contributors to this volume are a veritable multivoiced choir, counting almost fifty in number. They are younger and older, ordained and lay folk, newer believers and veterans of the faith. All have enjoyed some connection with the Kreiders over the years and share with them at least two common convictions: that the demise of Christendom offers God's people a fresh opportunity to be the faithful church, and that the Anabaptist stream of Christian history has a particular calling and unique role to play in helping to shape what that faithful church might look like.

On forming Christian habits in post-Christendom

There has been no attempt in this volume to set forth a list of *all* the Christian habits that will be necessary for the church living in a post-Christendom era.[11] We are only after all at the very front end of exploring where this new era will take us. Seeing tantalizing glimpses and hearing seasoned suggestions is a great way to start in charting a new course.

Dorothy Bass and Craig Dykstra refer to Christian habits practiced within the faith community as "rehearsing a way of life."[12] New communities experimenting with new habits and practices may initially feel that there is as yet precious little to rehearse. With time, however, "the physical artifacts, patterns of activities, and the language and story" embraced, practiced, and rehearsed by a faith community will begin to "embellish those objects with meaning."[13] That is why it is so crucial at this pivotal moment in history for the post-Christendom body of Christ to think prayerfully, creatively, and intentionally about what it means to be God's people in this time and place.

Old patterns of personal spirituality and community habits, rituals, programs, and techniques are fading away with the Christendom that created them, opening fresh space, according to Philip Sheldrake, for a deeper, more conscious "relationship with God, in Jesus Christ, through the indwelling of the Spirit and in the context

---

[11] Dorothy C. Bass, in *Practicing Our Faith: A Way of Life for a Searching People* (San Francisco: Jossey-Bass, 1997), identifies twelve "practices" that could potentially serve as a starter list, should someone choose to compile one. Her list includes honoring the body, hospitality, household economics, saying yes and saying no, keeping the Sabbath, testimony, discernment, shaping communities, forgiveness, healing, dying well, and singing our lives.

[12] Craig Dykstra and Dorothy C. Bass, "Times of Yearning, Practices of Faith," in *Practicing our Faith*, ed. Bass, 8–10.

[13] See Nancy T. Ammerman, *Congregation and Community* (New Brunswick, NJ: Rutgers University Press, 1997), 47.

of the community of believers."[14] The result, believes Sheldrake, will be a dynamic convergence of "theology, prayer and practical Christianity."[15] For British theologian Archbishop Rowan Williams, this marks the end of conventional spirituality as "merely the science of interpreting exceptional private experiences" and ushers in a more holistic reality that "must now touch every area of human experience, the public and social, the painful, negative, even pathological byways of the mind, the moral and relational world."[16]

This is of course the stuff of which Alan and Eleanor Kreider have been penning articles, delivering homilies, and conducting seminars for almost four decades. And their enthusiasm for a kingdom-size, shalom-shaped, missio-driven, God-breathed Reconciling Project has been contagious, spilling out across their years of ministry and off the pages of this collection of writings by the students, friends, and colleagues they have so richly inspired and blessed.

Thank you, Alan and Eleanor, for your exemplary lives, for your humble service, and for your vigilance and faithfulness to the task for which God has called and sent you.

---

[14] See Philip Sheldrake's chapter, "What is Spirituality?" in *Exploring Christian Spirituality: An Ecumenical Reader*, ed. Kenneth J. Collins (Grand Rapids, MI: Baker Books, 2000), 40.

[15] Ibid.

[16] In Rowan Williams, *The Wound of Knowledge: Christian Spirituality from the New Testament to St. John of the Cross* (London: Darton, Longman & Todd, 1979), 2.

3

Missio Dei
See God at work

Mission is central to theology. Many Christendom approaches to mission have enabled people to regard mission as an appendage to theology as a whole, a seedy subdivision of pastoral theology. In contrast, the missio Dei *invites us to see mission as central to the entire theological enterprise. It is central because all areas of theology have to do with God whose nature, passion, and determination are mission leading to the reconciliation of all people and things in Christ. The missio Dei is also central to the life of every church and every Christian. As Jürgen Moltmann has put it, "The whole congregation and every individual within it belong with all their powers and potentialities to the mission of God's kingdom."* [1]

To understand God's mission in the world we must understand the biblical concept of shalom. Christendom missionaries often made "peace with God" central to their evangelism. But they rarely mentioned the many facets of biblical shalom and the centrality of reconciliation to God's purposes. Now, after Christendom, the missio Dei restores multidimensional peace to the heart of all reflection about evangelism. More than that, it also sees God's shalom-making in all areas of life, where God is active and invites the collaboration of God's people. [2]

The missio Dei integrates mission with life—all aspects of life. In Christendom, mission was a specialized activity, carried out by special

---

[1] Jürgen Moltmann, *The Church in the Power of the Spirit: A Contribution to Messianic Ecclesiology* (New York: Harper and Row, 1977), 10.

[2] Willard Swartley, "The Evangel as Gospel of Peace," in *Evangelical, Ecumenical, and Anabaptist Missiologies in Conversation: Essays in Honor of Wilbert R. Shenk,* ed. James R. Krabill, Walter Sawatsky, and Charles van Engen (Maryknoll, NY: Orbis Books, 2006), 69–77.

*Christians on behalf of ordinary Christians. Further, most people saw
mission as having especially to do with the relationship of humans to God,
so mission and evangelism were often used as interchangeable terms. After
Christendom, in missio Dei understandings, evangelism is as necessary
as ever—God still invites people to be at peace with the God of love. But
the God of love is also the God of mission. And God's mission is broader
than evangelism. There are other areas that are also issues of God's mission—reconciliation between estranged enemies, restorative justice, community building, caring for the earth, ending the arms trade, growing
and distributing wholesome food, providing safe and ecologically modest
transport, healing bodies and minds—to name only a few.*

*Mission is broad, as broad as the Creator's concern, as broad as the
creation of which Jesus Christ is Lord. As we realize this about God, we
will increasingly join Andrew Kirk in affirming that "the life of work is
for almost all Christians the primary missionary frontier."[3] A product
of missio Dei thinking is that, after Christendom, the workplace may be
filled with Christians who decide what they do, and do what they do, in a
distinctive way because they know they are participating in God's mission.
And not only work, but also retirement, which can either be self-indulgent
or a participation in God's mission.*

*This approach may make mission seem so all-encompassing that it risks
becoming meaningless. And so discernment will be necessary. As Stephen
Neill once commented, "If everything is mission, nothing is mission."[4]
Neill's objection is a serious one. Missio Dei thinking can be vague and
slippery.[5] There are areas of God's action that some advocates of the missio
Dei may be tempted to view as old fashioned—some Christians committed*

---

[3] J. Andrew Kirk, "My Pilgrimage in Mission," *International Bulletin of Missionary Research* 28, no. 2 (2004): 73.

[4] Stephen Neill, *Creative Tension* (London: Edinburgh House Press, 1959), 81. William Abraham has usefully applied the same logic to evangelism: "If everything is evangelism, nothing is evangelism" (*The Logic of Evangelism* [Grand Rapids, MI: Eerdmans, 1989], 44).

[5] A. Camps, L. A. Hoedemaker, M. R. Spindler, and F. J. Verstraelen, *Missiology: An Ecumenical Introduction* (Grand Rapids, MI: Eerdmans, 1995), 162–65. See also George Sumner, "What's Anglican about Mission?" *Anglican Theological Review* 89, no. 3 (2007): 463: "The problem with this appealing term [*missio Dei*] has been that it remains devoid of content, and so is prone to be filled out with the favorite ideas of each user, in accordance with his or her ideological commitments."

to conflict mediation, for example, may be intolerant of evangelism and church planting.[6]

Other advocates of the missio Dei might be over-eager to construe sociopolitical movements as expressions of God's mission. It would not be the first time such a thing happened. Eusebius of Caesarea's sense of realized eschatology in the accession of the emperor Constantine I to the Christian faith has recent parallels in some Western Christians who enthusiastically embraced the Chinese Communist Revolution as "the foreordained answer to devout Christian prayers."[7]

The central question of discernment in each situation is, what is God doing? It does not follow that something is an expression of the missio Dei simply because it is novel and politically potent. Further, it does not follow that something is an expression of God's mission simply because it calls itself Christian. Alas, some Christian phenomena—including some forms of missionary activity—have in fact been impediments to God's mission. Remember, Jesus was scathing when he spoke about Jewish missionaries who "cross sea and land to make a single proselyte" whom they made "children of Gehenna" (Matt. 23:15). Likewise, it was in the very citadel of Jewish cultic life that Jesus became thoroughly angry and began to throw things about (Mark 11:15–17). So it is vital that we trust the Spirit to help us discern well what the missional God is doing, and what human actions collaborate with God's work. In contrast, it is crucial that we discern what God is not doing, and what human actions are deeply questionable and even violations of God's mission.[8]

....

---

[6] Jim Reapsome, "Holistic Reach," *Christianity Today* 51, no. 6 (June 2007), 73.

[7] Eusebius, *Oration in Praise of Constantine* (336), 2.3; 16.3–7; Lamin Sanneh, *Disciples of All Nations: Pillars of World Christianity* (Oxford: Oxford University Press, 2007), 282.

[8] Reprinted from *Worship and Mission after Christendom*, by Alan and Eleanor Kreider. Copyright © 2011 by Herald Press, Scottdale PA 15683. Used by permission.

⦂ Jonathan J. Bonk

To contribute to a celebrative piece for my good friends and exemplars Alan and Eleanor Kreider is a humbling honor indeed. Few among fellow travelers of my generation have so patiently, quietly, persistently, and effectually articulated, advocated, and modeled Christian habits in post-Christendom Europe. Although the Kreiders resided in the United Kingdom for the better part of their ministry, through their writing they have encouraged those of us who live and move in neo-Christendom United States to be Christ-ones in a society proudly suffused with "Christian" religiosity, strident nationalism, and unabashed militarism. This is a society, furthermore, whose "Christian" citizens yield obeisance to the presumably infallible hidden hand of the marketplace—a merciless idol that is satisfied with nothing less than the sacrifice of human beings and even the planet.

Shaped, defined, and conditioned within such an environment, our understanding of missio Dei is inevitably flawed and at times even misguided. Even the most theologically attentive among us can forget that God's mission in the world is through Jesus the Christ. Jesus not only gave his life to bring about the reconciliation of all creation with its Creator, he also showed us what God is like and how his followers should live and work and die in his Father's world.

So, how did *God* go about mission?

Let us imagine a council convened to lay plans for saving the world. The planet slipped out of its Creator's grasp when the first humans opted for alienation. Although God cannot compel reconciliation, God's love will not permit simply letting them go. But human beings are now scattered across five continents and speak thousands of languages. Hundreds of generations have come and gone. Those still alive retain only faint and often garbled recollection of who they are and how they came to be that way.

The logistical and communications challenges are immense. Fortunately, the Convener of this council has several advantages:

access will be no problem—the Convener is omnipresent; coherent, linguistically intelligible communications should be simplicity itself—the Convener is omniscient; and command of the methods and resources requisite to the task can hardly be insurmountable—the Convener is omnipotent.

So what does God do? Ignoring sensible options more consonant with divine ineffable majesty, God sends his only son into the world as an illegitimate child, born out of wedlock to a peasant mother and a carpenter stepfather, in a brutally occupied back eddy of an irresistibly powerful empire. While details of the birth are somewhat sketchy, it is known that the baby arrives not in the maternity ward of the best medical facility of his day, but in a stable, in the presence of an assortment of common barnyard animals.

These doubtful witnesses are joined by shepherds, so notoriously unreliable that their word is unacceptable as legal testimony. The child is born outside the power and privilege structures of the day. No reporters are present, and no cameras are on hand to capture the epochal act of the ages-long moral drama. Later, Eastern astrologers, known for their elaborately fantastic speculations about the future, acknowledge him as a promised king.

We know nothing of his early years, except that the "wise men" unwittingly jeopardize the child's life, forcing his parents to become refugees before their firstborn could even toddle. Herod—exercising the murderous prerogative of the powerful—seems to be more than a match for Mary's tiny son. What Jesus and his parents do when they finally return to Nazareth is not known. Joseph and Mary continue to have children—stepbrothers and stepsisters among whom Jesus is elder brother. Presumably Joseph and his sons work as carpenters. They are devout, no doubt attending a local synagogue and performing the requisite annual pilgrimage to the temple in Jerusalem.

As Jesus grows and develops, we are told that he has to learn obedience, just like any other child. Aside from his seemingly inconsiderate adolescent behavior when he remains behind in the temple debating, causing his frantic parents no end of worry about his whereabouts, we learn only that "Jesus became wise, and he grew strong. God was pleased with him and so were the people" (Luke 2:52; CEV). This is not an auspicious beginning for a great man.

Even for the last three eventful years of his life, Gospel accounts provide only fragmentary information on how he busies himself in missio Dei. Despite his mandate to save the world, he remains utterly parochial. Allowing himself to be interrupted again and again, he is willingly drawn into the wrenching personal plights of men and women from the social and ethical margins of society: blind beggars, cripples, sick children, anxious parents, diseased lepers, the psychologically deranged, disreputable women, tax collectors, and social pariahs.

He is a servant, and a servant's agenda is set by those served, he explains to his uncomprehending disciples (Matt. 20:25–28). Frequently attacked by devout religious leaders because of his scandalous reinterpretation of "their" sacred text and his oft-perceived cavalier application of Moses's law, Jesus appears astonishingly tactless in his encounters with those whose goodwill he should be assiduously cultivating. These keepers of the law are greatly relieved when, after sustained effort and no little expenditure of personal resources, they have this heterodox troublemaker crucified on a Roman cross between two thieves.

Yet today neither Caesar nor the Sanhedrin's "Who's Who" wields influence. Insofar as they are remembered at all, it is only as a detail in the story of the Servant of servants. For us North American Christians whose material privilege and its concomitant power and prestige exceed that of 90 percent of this planet's inhabitants, it is important to remember that God's ways and means have not changed, for God continues, even today, to prefer astoundingly anti-intuitive ways in accomplishing his divine purposes. The mission is God's, after all, not ours. And because we inhabit God's moral universe, close association with brute power, vast organizations, skillful administrations, and large sums of money are not the key, or even *a* key to God's eternal purposes for humankind.

Three observations about God's mission in Jesus

It is more about a way of life than about a way of t

This introduction leads me to several observations germane ᴛᴏ . topic. First, much of what we have come to associate with the category *Christian* derives not from the teachings of Jesus our Lord but from the elaborate, well-intentioned, highly ingenious use of the Hebrew and Christian scriptures to legitimate, facilitate, and sustain political and military power, and to secure those privileges issuing from the church's accommodation to power. The thinking and behavior of Western Protestants and Catholics alike reflect Christendom's emphasis on doctrinal precision over Christ's insistence on a way of life.

Our Lord's own criteria for determining those who are his more often had to do with *behavior* than with *doctrinal opinions* or *prescribed religiosity.* It is worth noting that in Jesus' pronouncements on the final judgment, doctrinal correctness plays little role in determining the fate of those standing before the Judge. Jesus suggests that it is those who are not even aware of what they were doing who enter the kingdom of heaven (Matt. 7:21–23; 25:31–46). As far as Jesus is concerned, *behavior,* not *doctrine* ("the demons believe") is the DNA that constitutes irrefutable proof of his paternity.

Orthodox belief does not necessarily produce kingdom behavior. Second, although many—especially in the United States—argue that conservative Christian religion is an essential component of societal health, recent studies show that the most secular Western countries are the least socially dysfunctional. This was the disappointing conclusion drawn by Paul Gregory in a paper published in the July 2009 issue of the online journal *Evolutionary Psychology.*[9] This conclusion was based on a comparison of twenty-five measures, including rates of homicide, incarceration, suicide, infant mortality, life expectancy, gonorrhea, syphilis, abortion, teen pregnancies, marriage duration, divorce, alcohol consumption, life

---

[9] "The Chronic Dependence of Popular Religiosity upon Dysfunctional Psychosociological Conditions," *Evolutionary Psychology* 7, no. 3 (July 2009): 398–441; www.epjournal.net.

satisfaction, corruption, income inequality, levels of unemployment, and scale of poverty.[10] In this country, well-meaning, politically powerful conservative Christians have consistently favored social policies that take from the poor so that the rich can keep more. Such policies make the United States an anomaly among the world's so-called developed nations. As Gregory explains,

> As a member of the 1st world the U.S. is an anomalous outlier not only in its religiosity, but in social, economic and political policies as well. Provided with comparatively low levels of government support and protection in favor of less restrained capitalism, members of the middle class are at serious risk of financial and personal ruin if they lose their job or private health insurance; around a million go bankrupt in a year, about half due in part to often overwhelming medical bills. The need to acquire wealth as a protective buffer encourages an intense competitive race to the top, which contributes to income inequality. The latter leaves a cohort mired in poverty. Levels of societal pathology are correspondingly high.[11]

Sadly, the nation whose conservative Christian citizens often speak of it as a beacon of light comes dead last among all of the countries examined. With the highest percentage of its citizens "absolutely believing in God" (63 percent), believing the Bible to be literally true (30 percent), participating in religious services regularly (39 percent), and engaging in prayer (60 percent), the United States achieved the lowest International Social Survey Program (ISSP) score of 0 out of a possible 10. By way of contrast, Sweden, Denmark, and Germany achieved scores of 9.7, 9.1 and 10, respectively.[12] How could this possibly be? What makes us such hypocrites? Given our own exaggerated sense of global worthiness, the results suggest astounding self-delusion at best, and unabashed self-serving hypocrisy at worst. "What good is it, my brothers and

---

[10] Ibid., Appendices C, D, E, F, G, 437–41.

[11] Ibid., 421.

[12] Ibid., 437, Appendix B.

sisters, if someone claims to have faith but has no deeds?" (James 2:14; NIV).

Christian habits should produce redemptive counter-cultural communities. And with this I come back to missio Dei, and my third observation. For the greater part of human history, according to our own scriptures, those whose faith has been *credited to them as righteousness* have had no uniform pattern of religious belief or practice, let alone knowledge of Jesus the Christ. As Jesus reminded his disciples, "many prophets and righteous people longed to see what you see but did not see it, and to hear what you hear but did not hear it" (Matt. 13:17; NIV). Jesus in no way diminishes the secure standing of these prophets and righteous men and women before God. Nor does he disparage their truncated systems of belief. He simply points out that those who see and hear Christ are more privileged.

God is not only here but God has always been everywhere, from before the foundation of the earth. And the crucified Lamb— our Lord—is there, and has been there from the creation of the world (Rev. 13:8). His incarnation in human time and flesh is the central act of the cosmic drama produced and directed by God. Each generation of human beings throughout the world and its uttermost parts appears briefly on the stage and then exits. Some exit not knowing of the larger script—unaware that the central act which was written before the foundation of the world is the one whereby all people in all times can make sense of the whole. But they are a part of God's drama, nevertheless.

God's grace has always been and will always be extended to the created order on the basis of mercy. And there is nothing in the Hebrew and Christian scriptures to suggest that this mercy is triggered solely by mental appropriation of insider information about mysterious doctrines. Whether the beneficiary of God's mercy is a follower of Jesus or simply a righteous person whose inchoate longing is to see what the followers of Jesus now more clearly see, mercy is a result of God's action, not ours. The examples of "the prophets and those leading righteous lives" are seen through the cross of

Christ—the spotless lamb of God who was "slain from the foundation of the world" (Rev. 13:8; AV), taking away the sins of the world.

This line of thinking has profound implications for our understanding of missio Dei. It also directly affects those of us who—because we are professionally religious people making a living from maintaining and promoting our several versions of orthodoxy—easily slip into the error of the Pharisees, reifying our self-justifying pieties to such an extent that God is reduced or removed altogether from our "religious" practices and preoccupations.

Even intellectually rigorous theologies of missio Dei do not necessarily give rise to faith communities marked by distinctively Christian habits! Jews, Muslims, and other monotheists generally recognize missio Dei. What they do not recognize is that "in Christ God was reconciling the world to himself" (2 Cor. 5:16–20). And to the extent that Christian behavior contradicts the ritualistic confession that Jesus is Lord, we subvert our active participation in God's unique way of transforming this world—of establishing his kingdom and asserting his will on earth, as in heaven. In effect, we infiltrate missio Dei as fifth columnists.

Christ-centered missio Dei should take us back to the original commission, not in some reductionist way to win converts, save people, or plant churches, but to serve our neighbors for Jesus' sake, making disciples who—with us—learn of and from Jesus. Dedicated to forming Christian habits, such communities become significantly and redemptively countercultural, palpable manifestations of a genuine "longing for a better country—a heavenly one. Therefore God is not ashamed to be called their God; indeed, he has prepared a city for them" (Heb. 11:16).

⋮ Matthew Krabill

The world has seen vast changes in the century since the celebrated Edinburgh Missionary Conference of 1910. Among many things, the last hundred years have brought a change in the center of gravity in the Christian world from the United States and Europe to

Africa, Asia, and Latin America—and a paradigm shift in how we think about global Christianity.

It is not coincidental that the current shift in global Christianity from north to south is occurring just when the direction of international migration from north to south is reversing. For the last five hundred years international migration has come from the same areas that have been the centers of the faith and primary sources of missionary agency. Now migrations are from the new heartlands of Africa, Asia, and Latin America to Europe and North America.[13] This trajectory reversal is a momentous one in Christian history: it marks the West as one of the changing frontiers in mission, and nonwestern Christian immigrants as the potential missionary sending force.[14]

If we take our cues from the Incarnation, we should not be surprised to discover that the new thing God is doing in the West is in many ways being carried out by immigrants from parts of the world noticeably absent at the Edinburgh 1910 conference—from Brazil, Korea, and Nigeria, for example. This unlikely turn of events follows what Jonathan Bonk identifies as the countercultural, anti-intuitive, and subversive way God chose to enter the world and by which today God continues to accomplish God's purposes.

If what is currently happening in Mennonite Church USA is any indication of a broader trend, then Christian immigrants are currently helping the post-Christendom church rediscover its "lost" Christian habits and practices by living out a missio Dei that integrates mission with all of life.

Consider, for example, Mennonite Church USA, a denomination facing a crisis— particularly with regard to its Anglo constituents—characterized by rapid aging and low birth rates, loss of membership, disengagement of young adults, loss of evangelistic fervor, and increased cultural assimilation. A 2006 churchwide membership profile revealed that the demographic make-up, lan-

[13] Jehu J. Hanciles, *Beyond Christendom: Globalization, African Migration and the Transformation of the West* (Maryknoll, NY: Orbis Books, 2008), 178.

[14] Wilbert R. Shenk, "Recasting Theology of Mission: Impulses from the Non-Western World," *International Bulletin of Missionary Research* 25, no. 3 (2001): 98.

guage of worship, religious and devotional expressions, theological perspectives, and missionary outlook of MC USA as a body are being decidedly influenced by a new influx of immigrants from nonwestern contexts.

I live in Southern California. Forty new congregations have been added to the Pacific Southwest Mennonite Conference since 1980. Ninety-five percent of today's conference members are new to the Mennonite church, 92 percent are "people of color," and 87 percent are foreign born.[15]

Furthermore, these immigrants are active in prayer and Bible study, and display an eagerness to develop and maintain relationships with nonbelievers, a desire to live communally, an openness to the Holy Spirit, and an inclination to combine evangelistic outreach with social action in the urban contexts where they live—contexts that demand attention to needs related to personal brokenness and to unjust social and political structures.[16]

Aligning ourselves with the missio Dei requires discernment in every age. Today any talk of the revitalization of the Western church must take into account nonwestern immigrants, because the habits and practices central to life beyond Christendom[17] lie in the hands of those not held captive by it.

⠒ Juliet Kilpin

Urban Expression is an urban mission agency that began in London, England, in 1997. It started as one response to the churches' lack of engagement with some of the most marginalized urban communities. Our hope was that through self-funding, risk-taking, kingdom-minded teams of volunteers, new expressions of church would take shape that make sense in those neighborhoods. We rebelled against the proliferation of manufactured models of church

---

[15] Jeff Wright, "Teaching Position or Conversation Starter?" *Mennonite Quarterly Review* 81, no. 3 (July 2007): 427.

[16] Conrad Kanagy, *Road Signs for the Journey: A Profile of Mennonite Church USA* (Scottdale, PA: Herald Press, 2007), 182–86.

[17] See Hanciles, *Beyond Christendom.*

being offered, and decided that Urban Expression should not be a model-based agency but rather a values-based one. And so began the quest to mine deep for Christ-centered values.

My husband Jim and I volunteered to lead the first team. At that time we had little awareness of Mennonite history, but with the help of Stuart Murray Williams, who had spearheaded the concept of Urban Expression, we asked what values should be core influences in the way Urban Expression would operate. On looking at the list we drew up, Stuart's response was, "These look a lot like Anabaptist values!"

From that point on, a relationship began with the few individuals we could find who shared these values and could help us understand their roots and history and flesh them out in practice. Several staff members at the London Mennonite Centre, including Alan and Eleanor Kreider, welcomed these non-Mennonite explorers and graciously accompanied us on our journey.

Alan Kreider states that he has "found North American Mennonite missionaries in Europe . . . using seven methods: fostering ministries, planting and working in churches, establishing study centers, advocating Anabaptist insights, promoting a Christian peace witness, networking widely, and participating in ecumenical relationships. Not all . . . have been involved in all seven of these, but some have."[18]

On reading this statement I am struck by two things. First, while there have been few North American Mennonite missionaries in Britain, there has been a steady growth in the number of British followers of Jesus who have responded to the call to be missionaries to Britain's underchurched, overcrowded, overlooked, yet potential-filled inner cities. Those who have chosen to partner with Urban Expression in this call have done so because of our values. To date, more than seventy adults have committed a minimum of

---

[18] See Alan Kreider, "West Europe in Missional Perspective: Themes from Mennonite Mission, 1950–2004," in *Evangelical, Ecumenical, and Anabaptist Missiologies in Conversation: Essays in Honor of Wilbert R. Shenk*, ed. James R. Krabill, Walter Sawatsky, and Charles van Engen (Maryknoll, NY: Orbis Books, 2006), 214. This passage appears also in the extract from the Kreiders' writings in the next chapter.

three years each in Britain, and others in the Netherlands have done so, too. I suspect that while most are networked within a variety of denominations, many of them, given the opportunity, would become Mennonite! As a compromise—and not knowing how to become Mennonite without joining the sole Mennonite congregation in the country—many of us are happy to simply say that we have "Anabaptist tendencies"!

Second, I am deeply encouraged that between all the various teams that have worked across six British cities and five Dutch towns to date, all seven methods that Alan refers to have been employed and practiced, with several teams managing to achieve some measure of all seven of the methods in one location. Alan is correct when he states that "this has been a costly approach to mission; it has been demanding for the missionaries."[19] Hence we have been grateful for the Anabaptist heritage our teams have been able to lean on when things get tough. The sacrificial, determined, gracious and peace-filled spirit of the Mennonite tradition has been for us both inspirational and motivational.

Alan goes on to say that "it is precisely the holism of our approach, which grows out of our Anabaptist-colored Christian faith and possibly our upbringing as Mennonites, that has been our best contribution to mission in Europe."[20] I am sure that this contribution is more far-reaching than the Kreiders know, and the determination to communicate with, educate, and inspire others to follow in this way has been hugely appreciated by many of us in Urban Expression.

---

[19] Ibid.

[20] Ibid.

II.
Mission

4

Holistic mission
Listen for God's call

The vision toward which we live is shalom. In shalom everything fits together—the spiritual and the social, even such "incompatibles" as justice and worship, evangelism and peacemaking. Many Christian traditions tell us that these don't fit together. Many political leaders try to keep them apart. Some Christian spokespersons give up politics for Lent. They admonish us to concentrate on eternal, "spiritual" questions, such as the afterlife. But Jesus and the early Christians remind us that the eternal life is happening now. "We know that we have passed from death to life because we love one another. Whoever does not love abides in death" (1 John 3:14; John 17:3).

This passage calls us to embody a different quality of social relationships now, to experience the justice, peace, and joy of God's kingdom now, to experience shalom now. This affects every area of our life, and God calls us to be involved in making it: "Blessed are the shalom-makers, for they shall be called God's children" (Matt. 5:9). No areas of life are excluded from God's shalom.

Of course all of us have blind spots. All of us Christians have blinkers. All of our church traditions have limited vision. Repentance and growth are necessary for us all. How can we keep growing as we see more and more of this vision? How can we fit it all together? Our conviction is that this will happen especially in worship. When we meet God, we will deeply know that we are God's loved sons and daughters, members of God's family. When we realize that the God who loves and forgives us is the God of shalom, then we will see anew, see more profoundly, see more comprehensively. God will give us a holistic agenda—the agenda of God's kingdom.

Humbled, moved, and animated by our encounter with God in worship, we will "seek shalom and pursue it" (1 Pet. 3:11) with reflexes that look like Jesus.[1]

. . . I have found North American Mennonite missionaries in Europe, over the past half century, using seven methods—fostering practical ministries, planting and working in churches, establishing study centers, advocating Anabaptist insights, promoting a Christian peace witness, networking widely, and participating in ecumenical relationships. Not all Mennonite missionaries in Europe have been involved in all seven of these, but many have.

This has been a costly approach to mission. It has been demanding for the missionaries. Mennonite workers have been involved not just in church planting but in planting peace churches. They have been involved not just in academic research and debate but in study plus helping international students who don't have credit ratings find housing. They have not just been involved with evangelicals but have also built friendships with Catholics and non-Christians. They have not simply established churches but have also attempted to build community.

I have wondered at times whether we missionaries would have been more productive if we had had a simpler, more focused approach. But I believe not. I think it is precisely the holism of our approach, which grows out of our Anabaptist-colored Christian faith and possibly our upbringing as Mennonites, that has been our best contribution to mission in Europe.[2]

....

---

[1] Alan and Eleanor Kreider, "Living toward a Vision: The Worship God Requires," speech at a conference sponsored by the Aslan Education Unit, Leeds, England, March 24, 1984.

[2] Reprinted from Alan Kreider, "West Europe in Missional Perspective: Themes from Mennonite Mission, 1950–2004," in *Evangelical, Ecumenical, and Anabaptist Missiologies in Conversation,* ed. James R. Krabill, Walter Sawatsky, and Charles Van Engen (Maryknoll, NY: Orbis Books, 2006), 214. Used by permission of the publisher.

⦂ Kim Tan

Mission should never need adjectives like *holistic* or *integral* to qualify it. After all, God's mission has always embraced *all* of creation, not just part of it. Indeed, the fact that so many people find it necessary to employ terms such as holistic or integral suggests that the church has deviated from the original norm. With that in mind, my contribution to this collection begins by outlining a holistic view of mission, then considers how we have deviated from it, and finally explores a number of ways for the church to recapture a more integrated approach to mission in today's world.

Holistic mission and the early church

Pentecost—a rushing wind, flames of fire, people speaking in tongues—triggered the questions that led to Peter's proclamation of the gospel and to the repentance and belief that followed. Most evangelicals would endorse the centrality of such proclamation for mission, while charismatic Christians might emphasize the supernatural signs that accompanied the proclamation. For me, however, the greatest miracle at Pentecost was that new believers sold their assets and shared their goods and daily meals with strangers who had become their newfound family members, creating a new community that, astonishingly, cut squarely across all existing racial, economic, and social lines.

The first "mission" campaign was thus truly holistic. Word, signs, and deeds, evangelism and social action, proclamation and demonstration, faith and works, belief and belonging—all went hand in hand. Belief meant far more than intellectual assent; it led to transformed behavior. Evangelism, too, led to both personal and social transformations—proof that good news had in fact been received as such! The result of this integrated approach to church life was that this new supernaturally generous community had a "wow" factor that attracted thousands to join them.

The early church grasped the comprehensive nature of the gospel, so it affected their work at the most fundamental levels. If you were a disciple, the church's emphasis on peace and enemy loving excluded you from becoming a charioteer, a soldier, or a magistrate.[3] This was whole-life discipleship with faith having an impact on every area of life.

Throughout church history radical groups emphasized making *disciples* rather than merely *converts.* In particular, the Anabaptists' holistic view of discipleship led to a vigorous determination to work out how doctrine affects practice, how faith is demonstrated in works, how word and deed match up. The result was a form of mission that included setting up communities with economic sharing, farming, crafts, and trades. For the early church and the radical groups, obedience to the Great Commission went hand-in-hand with the Great Commandment.

How and why holistic mission became reduced in meaning and scope

So why has this holistic view of mission been lost? I would like to suggest a number of reasons:

Hellenization. One might argue that much of Christian faith simply isn't Jewish enough. The Hellenistic culture surrounding the early church was steeped in the Greek philosophical worldview of dualism that posited a separation of sacred and secular, spiritual and physical. By contrast, Jewish faith was always much more integrated in its approach. God made the material world "and saw that it was good." Some Jews have even incorporated into their worship rituals the Asher Yatzar prayer, now more than two thousand years old, thanking God for proper toilet functions!

After Constantine's conversion, the influence of Greek thinking on the Jewish character of the early church accelerated. But Jesus was a Jew. And the Bible is a Jewish book written primarily by Jews from a Jewish point of view. Perhaps as part of our attempt to restore holism to our mission efforts we should recover something of the Jewishness of our faith and call our Lord by his real name, *Yeshua ben Yosef,* the Messiah, rather than Jesus Christ—a

---

[3] See Alan Kreider, *The Change of Conversion and the Origin of Christendom* (Harrisburg, PA: Trinity Press International, 1999).

name which for many people has been reduced to little more than a swear word.

From the Hellenistic worldview we have inherited a number of deviant tendencies. First, a tendency to *dichotomize* and *compartmentalize* life—into "social" and "spiritual" gospels where clergy do spiritual things, and laity don't; and into Sundays, when faith is alive, and weekdays, when faith is left in the parking lot outside the workplace.

Second, we *spiritualize* our faith when we should not. We forget that faith is not something we simply possess and profess but something we practice. By and large, the Christian churches have spiritualized away Yeshua's teachings and those of the Old Testament about wealth, the poor, and peacemaking into nonmaterial metaphors for richness or poverty of character, and the spirit and affability of fellowship.

Third, we often *individualize* our faith instead of thinking corporately, emphasizing *personal* holiness over *social* holiness.[+]

Professionalization of the clergy. The development of the clergy meant that "ordinary" believers lost a sense of responsibility for mission. The clergy get paid; it is therefore their job to do mission. The laity can thus retreat to attendance on Sundays and to tithing. Yet holistic mission requires the recovery of the priesthood of all believers for the proper exercise of body ministry in the world.

Fear of a liberal "social gospel." The "social gospel"—loosely understood as a Protestant movement that applied progressive ethics to social problems—has been the preserve of the liberal wing for so long that many respectable evangelicals avoid social engagement altogether, lest they be painted with a liberal brush. Happily, within the evangelical world, much has been done by John Stott and Rene Padilla and others to call the church to reengage with issues of injustice as part of the church's holistic mission.

Inheritors of distorted Pauline theology. Much Christian theology has placed an unfortunate wedge between Paul's writings

[+] See Alan Kreider, *Journey towards Holiness: A Way of Living for God's Nation* (Basingstoke, Hampshire, England: Marshall Pickering, 1986; Scottdale, PA: Herald Press, 1987).

and the synoptic Gospels, paying little attention to Paul's Jewishness and his understanding of the God of Israel's salvation plan. Furthermore, quasi-Pauline doctrines have been more frequently taught than some of Jesus' teachings such as the Sermon on the Mount, a dynamic that has led to the erroneous view that right belief is more important than right behavior. But the early church's primary manual for discipleship was the Sermon on the Mount. Right thinking, in the view of the earliest believers, has to result in right living. Thankfully, recent biblical scholarship has begun to correct popular misunderstandings on this matter by paying more attention to Paul's Jewishness and his first-century context.[5]

Holistic mission and Jubilee

What should be our understanding of holistic mission then? At the start of his ministry, according to Luke's Gospel, Yeshua goes back to words from Isaiah 61 to announce his mission: "The Spirit of the Lord (Adonai) is upon me; therefore he has anointed me to announce Good News to the poor; he has sent me to proclaim freedom for the imprisoned and renewed sight for the blind, to release those who have been crushed, to proclaim a year of the favor of Adonai" (Luke 4:18–19; Jewish New Testament). This was an unusual manifesto, highlighting the role of the Spirit and speaking of healing, yet using the language of the freedom fighters who wanted independence from Rome. It is a compelling mix of religious, political, social, and economic objectives. It is—in other words—holistic.

Compare this then with the narrow understanding of mission many Christians have today, stemming largely from a truncated interpretation of the Great Commission found in Matthew 28. Here, making disciples is essentially reduced to making converts, and both Matthew's understanding of the comprehensive scope of discipleship and the Luke 4 vision of mission that embraces social holiness, justice, and evangelism go largely missing.

---

[5] See especially the works of N. T. Wright, whose scholarship is readily available in popular books, articles, interviews, and his "For Everyone" New Testament commentary series published by SPCK and Westminster John Knox Press.

What does "good news to the poor" mean? And what is the year of the Lord's favor? Isaiah is referring to the Jubilee plan that God had instituted for Israel to carry out when they entered the promised land. This was a radical socioeconomic initiative that would have resulted in social holiness for the nation. It was an imaginative, humanitarian program involving a year's holiday to discourage exploitation of the land, animals, and slaves. Included here was a requirement to forgive debts, release slaves, and return to their original owners all properties bought in the previous forty-nine years. In addition to wealth creation, the plan also provided a blueprint for wealth distribution in order to develop and maintain a just society.

But the program failed. It was never carried out by the nation of Israel. Why? Most likely because it was simply too radical. Human effort alone could never succeed in realizing the Jubilee vision, because of the people's deep addiction to materialism. In fact, the Jubilee promise, that there would be no poor among you (Deut. 15:4), conditional on the nation's obedience (Deut. 15:5), was only finally fulfilled at Pentecost, and this, through the gift and power of the Holy Spirit (Acts 4:34).

In announcing his ministry, then, with the words from Isaiah 61, Yeshua was in effect saying that the Jubilee program was by no means dead. God was still in fact interested in a people characterized by social holiness, and Yeshua and his disciples were to be the agents for bringing this into being. The ministry of Yeshua and of the church must therefore be viewed from the perspective of Jubilee. This is vintage holistic mission.

Holistic mission is not evangelism done alongside social action, as if they were flipsides of a coin, with only one side visible at a time. No, it is more integrated than that, like a mixture of two cordials of concentrate poured into a pitcher to make fruit punch. It is where our evangelism results in social transformation and where our social action in turn leads to spiritual transformation. It is where whatever we do (see Col. 3:23)—work, evangelism or social action—bears witness to the grace of God leading to multidimensional transformation.

Because humans are multidimensional beings, mission too must be multidimensional. At the heart of this multidimensional holism is a vision of Jubilee characterized by shalom, offered by God, available to all. And at the heart of shalom is generosity, known and experienced first by those of us who have been recipients of God's extravagant grace and mercy, and then passed along through us to others whom God so passionately loves.

Holistic mission and creation mandate

Holistic mission recognizes work as part of God's intention for humanity. God put humans to work, first as gardeners, then as farmers. Work is not only meant for productivity but also as an expression of our creativity, as we are fashioned after the image of God. The absence of work—unemployment—is a mission issue. Holistic mission involves restoring God's image among the poor, and empowering them to work creatively.

Genesis also teaches us that God put humans in an environment where flourishing could take place. In this beautiful garden, people could develop their full potential as God had intended. Holistic mission is about imitating God by creating environments where human flourishing can take place, in our factories, offices, schools, homes, communities, and churches. Slums are not places conducive to human flourishing. Holistic mission means that humans need to be restored in their relationships with God, their neighbor, their environment, and with creation as a whole.

Holistic mission and discipleship

Holistic mission can only flow out of a holistic lifestyle, when we follow the Yeshua who is Lord of *all*, our time, our money, our talents. Not just our tithe, but *all* our resources. Not just our *spiritual* gifts, but *all* our gifts, whether they be musical, business, teaching, banking, or engineering.

To a packed audience, a well-known preacher once asked those who were "full-time Christian workers" to raise their hands. A smattering did. He asked the same question again, but louder. A few more hands were raised. A third time he asked, yet louder still, emphasizing "*full-time* Christian workers" and all hands went up.

The audience finally got the message. There is no such thing as a part-time Christian.

The key phrase in Leviticus "before the Lord" is repeated some seventy times. Israel was instructed to do everything "before the Lord"—farming, cleaning, hairdressing, teaching, banking . . . *everything* "before the Lord" in order that we may glorify God through everything that we do. Our calling will not permit us to leave our faith in the parking lot. We must take it with us, into the office space and out to the marketplace.

In the Sermon on the Mount, Yeshua explains the basics of mission using three word pictures—salt, light, and yeast. Salt preserves and flavors. Light exposes darkness and shows the way. Yeast transforms inedible flour into delicious bread. The heart of mission calls us to be all three of these in our varied spheres of influence—at work; among family members; in our local communities; in business, the arts, media, and politics.

In recent years, a "Business as Mission" movement has emerged in Britain. It has antecedents in the original goals of many earlier companies such as Boots (the pharmacy chain), and Guinness (the brewery), to name two. I contend that for those called and gifted in this area, it is less helpful to think of business as mission, and more helpful to simply see that business *is* mission. In the same way, for those called to politics, politics *is* mission. And for still others in our faith communities, art *is* mission, hairdressing *is* mission, and banking *is* mission. In short, for those of us committed to God's shalom-making project, holistic, integrated mission is about living out our discipleship in *every area of life* to which we have been called.

Holistic mission, the poor, and the church

The poor, like all other human beings, have been created in the image of the God. They have creativity, talents, and abilities. What they do not always have are opportunities and hope. They often live in environments that are not conducive to human flourishing.

Poverty is the absence of choice and freedom. Holistic mission must involve restoring dignity to those in poverty, setting them free so they have choices, improving their living environment so they can flourish, and creating job opportunities so their creation in the image of God can be expressed through the work they do to the glory of their Creator.

God has given to the church the task of holistic mission. The future of this mission in local faith communities is twofold. First, it involves planting churches that are caring and generous Jubilee communities, committed to transforming their neighborhoods and environment. Such churches, second, will work to call forth and equip holistic missional disciples to be agents of the Jubilee kingdom wherever God places them, daily living out the values of the Beatitudes by following the One who came not to be served but to serve.

⋮ Lesley Misrahi

In 1975 I spent a summer volunteering at a Mennonite foyer for foreign students in Brussels. While there, I attended a worship service and heard a young preacher deliver his first sermon. I have never forgotten some of his words: *Un ventre vide n'a pas d'oreilles.* Alan and Ellie Kreider, with strong ties to the French-speaking world, will know the meaning of that expression: "An empty belly has no ears." It is a reminder to all of us that holistic mission means addressing the person as a whole.

As Kim Tan decries, mission has often been reduced to attempts at trying to win someone to a faith that divorces the spiritual from other aspects of life, while asserting that this will solve all other pressing problems. Such an approach can damage by disregarding others' full humanity, sullying the name of Jesus, and perhaps even wounding ourselves.

This chapter's title asks us to form the habit of listening for God's call. As Christians we are called to rejoice with those who rejoice, and to mourn with those who mourn (Rom. 12:15). To overlook or override that God-given sense of empathy in order to make converts of other people can be untrue to ourselves and to the fruit of our learning, gained through difficult times when it appeared that God did not meet our every need.

Alan and Ellie have never spent time counting converts, but their influence has been enormous nonetheless. They have enriched the lives of many, not by attracting people to themselves, but by turning people toward Jesus. They have obeyed the Great Commission by making disciples and teaching them "the agenda of God's kingdom."

Not only should mission relate to each person in a holistic way, it should also attempt to reach people of all varieties. Holistic mission requires a plural approach, multivoiced and from many life experiences. A diverse mission team is helpful but not enough. If "it takes a village to raise a child,"[6] then it requires a community to raise a disciple. Such a community is possible only when we turn to God in worship, are empowered by the Holy Spirit, and willingly learn the disciplines of shalom-making because we know ourselves to be God's beloved children. As Stanley Hauerwas has noted, "we do not learn about the demands of the kingdom by learning about freedom and equality; rather we must first experience the kingdom if we are even to know what kind of freedom and equality we should desire."[7]

Holistic mission is demanding, emotionally and intellectually, and seldom produces megachurches. The congregation Alan and Ellie founded, almost as a by-product of their many-faceted work in London, has struggled to survive beyond their personal inspiration. Yet, the holistic and Christ-centered vision they taught and lived continues in a small community striving to enable people, as Kim Tan has accurately highlighted, to be "agents of the Jubilee kingdom wherever God places them."

Alan's description of North American Mennonite mission activities in Europe reflects the relationships these missionaries initiated and fostered with "the whole person." In more recent years, as mission societies' resources have diminished, there has been less room for this broad approach. I believe this reality will hinder the reach of Anabaptism, leaving the field open to efforts more charac-

---

[6] African proverb, famously quoted by Hilary Clinton.

[7] Stanley Hauerwas, *The Hauerwas Reader*, ed. John Berkman and Michael Cartwright (Durham, NC: Duke University Press, 2001), 389.

terized by a prosperity gospel than by Jesus' manifesto delivered at
the outset of his public ministry in Nazareth.

⋮ Joe Liechty

Alan writes, "I think it is precisely the holism of our approach,
which grows out of our Anabaptist-colored Christian faith and possibly our upbringing as Mennonites, that has been our best contribution to mission in Europe." Having been the beneficiary of that
holism many times over, I agree and I am grateful.

There are, of course, holes aplenty in Mennonite holism. Some
of these blind spots, as Alan and Eleanor call them, only become
visible to Mennonite missionaries as they are revealed to us in mission contexts. One of those absences has been reconciliation. This
gap may seem perplexing, because reconciliation has become in
recent decades so prominent a peace theme, and Mennonites are
known for our peace witness. In truth, however, our peace thinking and action have been dominated for centuries by the theme of
resistance. For sixteenth-century Anabaptists, this was resistance,
sometimes unto death, to state efforts to impose religious confor-
mity. In the centuries since, Mennonites' peace witness centered
on conscientious objection to military duty. In these circumstances,
pacifism, especially in the form of resisting military participation,
was the dominant expression of Mennonite commitment to peace.
In terms of peace, holism is a recent development.

So it was in 1981 that I used my first speaking invitation in
Ireland to present a biblical rationale for pacifism. I was addressing the Student Christian Movement, a congenial group committed to peace and justice, and they received me politely and even
with warmth. The chairperson's concluding remarks, while kind,
left little doubt, however, that pacifism was well and good only if
it did not preclude occasional violence—just and necessary, even if
regrettable—by and for the oppressed. It was the first instance of
what became a common experience—encounters with Irish Christians radically committed to peace who nevertheless shied away
from pacifism.

Making pacifism the foundation on which to build shared work for peace in Northern Ireland might be a difficult task, it seemed. Neither did it prove necessary. In the mid-1970s, at the height of "the Troubles," the Catholic Church and the (Protestant) Irish Council of Churches appointed a high-level Working Party on Violence. Their superb analysis, published in 1976 as *Violence in Ireland: A Report to the Churches*, treated pacifism as an option with great integrity—in fact, the Working Party included both Protestant and Catholic pacifists within its ranks.

Pacifists and just war advocates did not need to settle their differences to work together effectively, however, because all could agree that despite past and current injustices suffered by Catholics, "there is no justification in the present situation in Ireland for the existence of any para-military organizations," and that "the State must avoid, to the utmost possible extent, any element of unnecessary destructiveness when it uses force to restrain the violent."[8] They captured a broad agreement, though not quite a consensus, among Irish Christians. This stance was peace-minded without requiring pacifism, and it proved to be a durable foundation for much creative peace work.

In the early years then, when our little Mennonite group in Dublin cast about for a theme that might guide our work, we settled on reconciliation. We took our rationale and guidance not from Mennonite theologians but from writers such as Jean Vanier, the Canadian Catholic founder of the L'Arche communities, and above all from Irish Christian organizations committed to reconciliation, such as the Corrymeela Community (founded in 1965), the Irish School of Ecumenics (1970), and later the Evangelical Contribution on Northern Ireland (1987). These groups, others they inspired, and independent groups working from similar premises generated much action and thought. Out of it grew a sophisticated sense of what reconciliation means and requires.

---

[8] Joint Group on Social Questions, *Violence in Ireland: A Report to the Churches*, rev. ed. (Belfast: Christian Journals Limited; and Dublin: Veritas Publications, 1977), 90, 10.

Reconciliation was a great fit with Mennonite holism, and over time, Mennonites would contribute to reconciliation work in Ireland. First, however, we needed to make friends and be taught by them. Later we would learn that Mennonite mission and service workers around the world were having similar experiences, as our friends and coworkers helped us fill some of the holes in Mennonite holism.[9]

In the Kreider excerpt featured at the beginning of this chapter, Alan and Eleanor anticipate that God will give us a holistic agenda "especially in worship," where "we will deeply know that we are God's loved sons and daughters, members of God's family." In my experience, the learning came sometimes in worship, more often in shared work, but always in sacred relationship with the friends and partners God has given us.

---

[9] For an account of the development of Mennonite mission work in Ireland from 1970 to 1998, and for parallel stories from many locations, see Cynthia Sampson and John Paul Lederach, eds., *From the Ground Up: Mennonite Contributions to International Peacebuilding* (New York: Oxford University Press, 2000).

5

Social holiness
Join God's journey

Holiness, according to the Bible, is on the move. There is something pro-pulsive, forward-looking, about it. It is the realization of God's "uncon-ditional will, his royal rule." [1] *Holiness shows itself in action, shattering all resistances to God's sovereignty and liberating women and men from all forms of bondage. In the Exodus God showed himself to be "majestic in holiness" (Exod. 15:11), and the Exodus is a pattern for his people (Lev. 11:45). Just as God invites his people to enter into his character, so God also calls us to take part in his holy actions.*

God's holiness is thus not something that is changelessly sublime. It is not something that is legalistically separate. It is not self-preoccupied in its concern for its own wholeness. Any of these on its own is a distortion of holiness, for it is static and small-minded. God's holiness, in contrast, is cosmic in scope and always in motion. It is historical, in world as well as "church" history. It is understandable, therefore, that when the Holy One confronted Isaiah, he did not just call him to be a missionary ("Here am I; send me!" [Isa. 6:8]). There was to be something distinctive about his mis-sion. He was to speak Yahweh's word in the political realm where Yahweh would unfold his historical plan. Similarly, when Peter had a rooftop vision of common and unclean foods, God was not simply trying to change Peter's diet. God was doing no less than preparing him to be midwife at the birth of a transnational holy nation (Acts 10).

God's holiness is thus en route. It is an energizer of all actions that point to the completion of his project, the coming of a recreated cosmos.

---

[1] Hans Wildberger, *Jesaja* 1, Biblischer Kommentar; Altes Testament 10, no. 1 (Neukirchen-Vluyn: Neukirchener Verlag, 1965–72), 249.

What a vision! God, though transcendently "other," is revealing himself to men and women. God is calling us to occupy a special place—that of a nation under his kingship. He is implanting in us the vision and reality of wholeness. And God is energizing us to be participants in his own all-embracing historical plan. One is speechless at the magnificence of it.[2]

....

⋮ David Nussbaum

In June 1983, Margaret Thatcher was re-elected prime minister of the United Kingdom, with a large majority of 144 in the elected chamber of the British parliament. This political victory owed much to British military success in the Falklands War of 1982, and to the emerging economic success Thatcher's government had been building from the decline it had inherited on coming into office four years earlier (although unemployment remained at record levels). In Western Europe, American nuclear missiles were being deployed; in particular, nuclear-armed cruise missiles arrived at Greenham Common in the UK in 1983.

Internationally, United States president Ronald Reagan had proposed his Strategic Defense Initiative (popularly known as Star Wars), had described the Soviet Union as an evil empire, and was re-elected with a large majority in 1984. Meanwhile, Yuri Andropov had taken over from Leonid Brezhnev as leader of the USSR in 1982, and after his death in 1983 was succeeded by Konstantin Chernenko for a year in early 1984. Both pursued the second Cold War. It was only in 1985 that Mikhail Gorbachev came to power, and the changes that started with *glasnost* ("openness") and *perestroika* ("restructuring") ensued, leading four years later to the fall of the Berlin Wall and the subsequent collapse of the USSR.

---

[2] Reprinted from *Journey towards Holiness: A Way of Living for God's Nation*, by Alan Kreider. Copyright © 1987 by Herald Press, Scottdale PA 15683. Used by permission.

The world of the 1980s
and the relevance of social holiness

This world of the 1980s was the backdrop for an invitation to Alan Kreider to speak at the Baptist Mainstream conference in 1984 on the subject of social holiness. The milieu for Alan's engagement with this theme could hardly have been more pertinent; discussion around social, political, economic, and military issues was at the center of national and international news. In the UK the contentious miners' strike in 1984–85 filled television screens and newspapers with daily images of violence and discord, and the Thatcher government was privatizing formerly nationalized industries and pulling back the boundaries of the state.

The issues were being fiercely debated, and as the popular re-elections of Thatcher and Reagan indicated, militaristic rhetoric and action were meeting with popular acclaim. It was not an easy time to be advocating for shalom, perhaps especially in the UK, when in October 1984 the Irish Republican Army almost succeeded in its attempt to wipe out the cabinet and much of the government in a bomb attack at the Conservative Party conference in Brighton. Yet the need for shalom on a global scale was starkly demonstrated by the Ethiopian famine of 1984–85, which inspired the 1984 hit single "Do They Know It's Christmas?" and the Live Aid concert the following year.

In this context, Alan studied and reflected, talked and taught about social holiness. And of course he wrote. One of the reasons I have dwelt on the external background is because Alan does so in his writing on this theme. Not that the book makes much acknowledgement of the contemporary context in which its content was formed. In fact, in the introduction to *Journey towards Holiness*, Alan specifically writes, "I want to write primarily, not about the contemporary world, but about the Bible."[3]

But as he takes us through the narrative, he draws our attention to the external environment in which the people of God, whether in Old and New Testament times, or indeed in the history of the

---

[3] Kreider, *Journey towards Holiness*, 12.

Christian church, have had to make their decisions about how they will live. This approach helped to bring the biblical material alive, but it still had to be made relevant to the lives of contemporary people.

Social and holiness: Do these words belong together?

Journey towards Holiness was published in 1986. It used material developed by Alan, myself, and others for teaching as part of the Cross-Currents program of the London Mennonite Centre—specifically a one-day seminar entitled "Social Holiness." With my own Christian roots in Methodism, I appreciated Alan's acknowledgement of one origin of this phrase: John Wesley's contention that there can be "no holiness but social holiness."[4]

Holiness is a big word, but a word Western culture had largely domesticated and diminished to fit the realm of the private and personal. Actually, the conjunction of "holiness" and "social" may have created cognitive dissonance for some Christians. If anything, that was our intention. Part of the purpose of the teaching, the writing, and the seminar was to associate aspects of people's thinking and actions that had all too often been disconnected. One element of the foundation for the book is that it addresses basic human concerns—protection and provision, the bottom rungs of Abraham Maslow's hierarchy of needs.[5]

One way we worked to bring these connections alive was through teaching, and particularly by the use of case studies. Alan and I developed and presented the Cross-Currents seminar on Social Holiness using his material supplemented by case studies produced primarily by me. At the time I was working in the training department of the accountancy firm Price Waterhouse and was finding out about how effective adult learning happens. So I got permission to use methods I had learned at Price Waterhouse as a framework around which to devise and document the case study approach we applied in the Social Holiness seminar. The case study materials,

---

[4] John Wesley, preface to *Hymns and Sacred Poems*, 1739.

[5] Abraham Maslow, *Motivation and Personality* (New York: Harper and Row, 1954).

along with the seminar visuals, were made more widely available, and are advertised on the last page of *Journey towards Holiness.*[6]

In addition to presenting the Social Holiness seminar at the London Mennonite Centre, Alan and I, sometimes with Ellie too, took it to some other churches and centers around the UK. The case studies enabled us to get participants in a typical daylong seminar to address what social holiness might mean when applied to practical situations, and to think about what their own journey toward holiness might entail in practice—not just in terms of spiritual disciplines but as it might affect the way they dealt with practical questions of protection and provision.

The case studies presented scenarios and required groups of seminar participants to make decisions. The subjects addressed included a physical threat to life, business decisions in a recession, employment opportunities, pension planning, postgraduate research options, redundancy prospects, and health-care choices. The scenarios developed as participants made their initial choices, and then the consequences of these choices confronted them. We found that groups often continued talking about the issues raised by the cases well after the seminar content was supposed to have moved on. The case studies helped demonstrate how the call to social holiness affects our jobs and savings, the way we handle our money and view the enemy.

So the case studies built on the material now in the book, and stimulated and enabled people to address what living in a holy way might mean when they faced hard decisions and challenges to conventional sources of security. The case studies recognized that the world is a complex, unholy place, and they did not lead to easy answers. Rather they presented dilemmas, as the events of our lives often do. But they also stimulated people to face into the implications, raised in Alan's teaching and writing, of God's demand that we Christians be holy, as God is holy. So the call was, and is, to transformation; or as the subtitle to the book has it, to "a way of living for God's nation."

---

[6] Alan Kreider and David Nussbaum, *Social Holiness—A Cross-Currents Study Guide* (London: London Mennonite Centre, 1987).

The balloonist's perspectives twenty-five years later

The cover of *Journey towards Holiness* has a picture of a colorful hot air balloon traveling over rolling English countryside. This photo picked up Alan's verbal picture in the second part of the book, where in chapter 4 he likens himself as author to a balloonist, wanting to travel high enough to see the overall contours yet low enough to examine some features more carefully, and at a speed such that things become neither stalled nor blurred. The balloonist becomes a recurrent image in the book and is picked up again at the end.

What perspective might we gain now, from the perspective of a balloonist surveying the twenty-five years since the book's publication, on the social holiness theme about which Alan wrote, and which he, Ellie, and others spoke about, discussed, and explored? What changes have there been?

Embracing the social. Much of the evangelical community, which was then instinctively in favor of holiness, has embraced more of the social, at least in the UK. Particularly in the more charismatic parts of that section of the church, engagement with social issues has grown, along with greater conviction that this dimension is part of the Christian gospel. The picture is not uniform, of course, but changes in the content of an initiative such as Spring Harvest (a weeklong holiday-based family teaching program in the UK that attracts 50,000 people each year) illustrate the way the agenda has moved to be more aligned with the some of the perspectives of *Journey towards Holiness*. Alan and Ellie's work and teaching, often mediated and amplified by others, has been one of many factors contributing to this change.

Embracing holiness. On the other hand, there seems to have been far less embracing of holiness by those on the Christian spectrum who were instinctively more comfortable with the social. A relatively recent upsurge of interest in "new monasticism" has been characterized in the main by what has been termed "monasticism lite"—seeking to enjoy the benefits of the lifestyle without having to embrace the poverty, the chastity, and the obedience.

Holiness and the need for protection. Recent decades have seen a significant change in what people in the UK and USA think they need physical protection from. In the mid-1980s it was nuclear attack and (in the UK and other parts of Europe, at least) domestic/separatist bombings. Today, in the early twenty-first century, concern has turned to international terrorism. Even war is associated in the public mind with terrorism, since the onset of what George W. Bush dubbed a "war on terror."

Nevertheless there has been change in how Christians and others in the UK view war, especially since the 2003 invasion of Iraq. Questioning of Christian participation in and support for war has grown, along with increased acceptance of pacifism as a—though not the—legitimate Christian position. But because so many of the suicide attacks have been the work of individuals inspired by Islamic teachings, the emotions around the threats from the new international terrorism differ significantly from those associated with the threats of the 1980s.

There is little in *Journey towards Holiness* about suicide attacks, though if Alan were writing now, perhaps he would explore one of the biblical stories that probably is most like a suicide attack—the death of Samson in causing the death of large numbers of Philistines, as recorded in Judges 16. This is a challenging passage, since this suicide bomber is a member of the people of God. I wonder how Alan might have developed that story for us.

Holiness and the need for provision. Turning to the theme of provision: among Christians in the UK in the 1980s one saw considerable interest in exploring radical alternative lifestyles. These often involved some form of communal living, sometimes with the "common purse" of financial pooling. Twenty-five years on, this interest has receded. While there are forms of Christian community, these have generally become less radical and more culturally assimilated.

An interesting, if sometimes—like the original Anabaptists—controversial exception would be the "modern Jesus army," or Jesus Fellowship. This group has been influenced significantly by Anabaptist thinking. As one of its leaders put it in 1995, "the Anabaptist connection is one of the strands of tradition we do recognize."[7] With its finances described on Wikipedia as "socialist,"[8] its practices can be seen to express both the social and the holiness elements of Jesus' teaching.

Returning to the biblical narrative, the source of our journey toward holiness. Finally, a noticeable change over the twenty-five years since *Journey towards Holiness* was written is a decline in familiarity with the biblical narratives, among the population generally, and also among Christians. Alan's approach was to retell the stories of God's people from the Bible, reminding his readers of what many of them already had some familiarity with. Today he could not assume that such acquaintance with the biblical text would be widespread among his readers, as the practices of regular Bible reading, biblical preaching, and group Bible studies have declined. Yet the consequence of this change is to make Alan's approach all the more crucial—to tell and retell the biblical narratives in ways that connect with the hearers. This is an even more essential part of forming Christian habits in the increasingly post-Christendom world of the 2010s.

⋮ Sally and Jim Longley

Alan and Ellie Kreider's impact has been felt around the world, in South Africa and Australia, among other places. They embody both personal holiness and social holiness, demonstrating in practice that the two are inseparable.

I (Sally) first encountered Alan when he was leading a chapel service at what is now London School of Theology. I was studying theology there, and would later return to South Africa and chaplaincy work at the universities. The clarity with which Alan pointed to the call for followers of Jesus not to trust in chariots but rather to trust in the name of the Lord came as a great shock. Thus began my personal journey, which included a dramatic paradigm shift from a

---

[7] http://www.jesus.org.uk/vault/articles_probing.shtml.

[8] http://en.wikipedia.org/wiki/Jesus_Army.

belief in the use of force to achieve justice in South Africa. Lengthy discussions with Alan and Ellie helped me see with new eyes how to follow Jesus in trusting in God.

In the 1980s the struggle to end apartheid was coming to a head. It was a dark and violent time as the Botha government became increasingly hard-line, detaining thousands without trial, and "eliminating" leaders who opposed the regime. In this environment Alan and Ellie's embodiment of social holiness was key in helping me discern how to be a follower of Jesus in such a crucial time.

In our time with the Kreiders at the London Mennonite Centre, and in their visits in our home in Sydney, and during our study at Associated Mennonite Biblical Seminary in Elkhart, Indiana, the close accord between their teaching and personal lifestyle gave reality to their call to enter into the character of the God of the Exodus and take part in God's holy actions.

Of particular significance for me (Jim) was Alan's encouragement to work through a major essay reflecting on my ten years as a member of Parliament and government minister in Australia. This essay, "Politics as a Mission of Peace," used the structure of John Howard Yoder's book *Body Politics*[9] to engage with scripture, Yoder's work, my own understanding, and perspicacious discussion with Alan. To speak Yahweh's holiness in the political realm is no mere verbal exercise but involves a much deeper commitment to action, both societally and in one's own life. The contemporary preoccupation with outcomes of political action tends to overlook the imperative that unless the process—both structural and personal—has integrity, the outcome will be flawed. Holiness is both inward/personal and external/societal. This key Anabaptist understanding is evinced in the Kreiders' work.

That "God's holiness is thus en route," that we are on a journey, rapidly becomes evident in our own life experience and our understanding of how, what, and why we speak into our society's situation. The end does not justify the means, because the ends are

---

[9] John Howard Yoder, *Body Politics: Five Practices of the Christian Community before the Watching World* (Nashville, TN: Discipleship Resources, 1992).

not static and so the means become ends. Following Jesus requires that we exercise the same epistemic and immanent humility that was Jesus' stance in engaging with the political process.

Alan and Ellie have illustrated to us in their writing and their lives that Jesus is the body language of God, and Alan and Ellie themselves walk with a posture of holy social servanthood.

⦂ Anna Geyer

Social holiness addresses the relationship between our ritual worship and our daily worship. It addresses how our Sunday morning life informs our life during the week. It addresses how our love for God informs our love for our neighbor.

Working out what social holiness looks like is messy and risky and requires us to let go of control, to trust that God will provide for and protect us as we make love for God and neighbor our primary concern.

Joe is teaching a class at the University of Iowa on social entrepreneurship—that is, business that addresses social concerns. His vision is both local and global. Joe is deeply concerned about the way the United States is involved in Iraq, Pakistan, and Afghanistan. He is unconvinced that peace can be achieved by war. His vision is to develop wind power in these countries: if we could assist in electrifying villages and provide heat and sanitation, it would take away their reason for hating us. It would build relationships and empower their independence.

In the context of a "war on terror," it may feel risky to let go of military defense. Where do we place our trust? How do we love our neighbor?

An issue closer to home, at least here in rural Iowa, is the contentious matter of hog confinements. If a hog farmer needs large-scale production to maintain his business, and his neighbors are angry about the smell, how are they to get along? These dynamics have created rifts in our community. One man went so far as to buy land near him, put an easement forbidding confinements on it, and then sell it again. He was eager to protect his air.

Two others have worked at these pressures differently. Phil began building a confinement. Several neighbors were angry and tried to stop it. Gary heard about the plan and chose not to get angry. When neighbors complained to him, he tried to diffuse their frustrations, never responding in a way that demeaned Phil. Phil planted trees around his hog confinement in an effort to minimize odor, and he offered to add enzymes to the pit when the smell got bad. But the enzymes were not as effective as promised. Gary was honest about the problem, yet he and Phil have maintained a respectful relationship.

When Phil was considering building a second confinement, he came to Gary with questions. How often was the odor a problem? How bad was it? How would he feel about a second confinement? Gary answered honestly and admitted that if a second confinement would make the smell twice as bad, he wouldn't want it. Phil decided not to build the second building.

What kind of love does it take to live at peace with someone whose business affects your comfort in profound and permanent ways? And what kind of trust does it take to limit your business because of your concern for your neighbor? These two men have been willing to hold their own comforts and needs more loosely in order to maintain their relationship.

6

Pacifism
Cultivate God's peace

The pacifist Christian senses a call to participate in a new world that God is building, and to invite the old world to join in.

To get to the new world, one must begin to see things differently . . . For Jesus' "hard sayings" cannot be taken piecemeal; they all fit together. And they not only apply to violence (unfortunately, many pacifists are strict interpreters solely of Jesus' teachings on violence!); they also lead to radical approaches to other areas of life, such as leadership and material possessions. The comprehensiveness of conversion, which freed the early Christians from the various forms of bondage of their former life, was well expressed by Justin Martyr, who in AD 165 was beheaded in Rome:

> *Those who once rejoiced in fornication now delight in continence alone; those who made use of magic arts have dedicated themselves to the good and unbegotten God; we who once took most pleasure in the means of increasing our wealth and property now bring what we have into a common fund and share with everyone in need; we who hated and killed one another and would not associate with men of different tribes because of [their different] customs, now after the manifestation of Christ live together and pray for our enemies and try to persuade those who unjustly hate us, so that they, living according to the fair commands of Christ, may share with us the good hope of receiving the same things . . . [Christ's] sayings were short and concise, for he was no sophist, but his word was the power of God (Justin,* First Apology *14).*

Of course, to live like this is to flout the accepted wisdom of self-preservation. Without material and military strength, one in one's helplessness is forced to depend on God for provision and protection. The consequences of this are unknowable . . . If faithfulness to Christ's teachings brings suffering and the cross, that is only what he promised us, along with his all-sufficient grace (2 Cor. 12:9).

On the other hand, pacifist Christians are convinced that God still does work miracles of provision and protection; and . . . they have collected stories of incidents in which God has vindicated his people's unworldly-wise fidelity—antagonists have behaved inexplicably; new methods of nonviolent resistance have been fruitful; enemies have been reconciled.[1]

What pacifists will be called to do in specific circumstances can thus not be predicted. The rules governing their action are less detailed than those of the just war doctrine; guiding their behavior is a simple positive command (Love your enemy!) with its corresponding negative command (Do not kill), applied by prayer and the discernment of their communities of faith.

These commands will make it impossible for pacifists to hold certain jobs. They will find it impossible to work in the armed forces, in defense-related industries and research, and in the military branches of the civil service. They will likewise not be able to hold political office that might require them to order the taking of life . . . But pacifists should be reluctant to tell others what to do. After bearing witness to their understanding of scripture, they should leave the application of their witness to the Spirit's work in the other's conscience. As the early Quaker George Fox told the newly converted gentleman William Penn, who had asked whether he must stop wearing his sword, "Wear it as long as you are able!"

The main concern of pacifist Christians, however, must not be avoiding "no-go areas"; it must be finding areas in which they can be peacemak-ers, *doing positive and distinctive things that will bring in the newness of God's kingdom. Since these will often be new ventures, on the fringes of society, they are hard to categorize. An old-age pensioner goes to live*

---

[1] See A. Ruth Fry, *Victories without Violence* (Santa Fe: Ocean Tree Books, 1986); Elizabeth H. Bauman, *Coals of Fire* (Scottdale, PA: Herald Press, 1954); Cornelia Lehn, *Peace Be with You* (Newton, KS: Faith and Life Press, 1980); and Philip Hallie, *Lest Innocent Blood Be Shed* (New York: Harper and Row, 1979).

in Derry, where both Protestant and Catholic paramilitaries discover that he, in his defenselessness, can be a trusted intermediary. A history student decides to do research into the largely unchronicled story of nonviolent social change. A theology student, fired by a gospel vision of reconciliation, decides to establish a Christian conflict resolution service. A scientist—aware that 90 percent of the research scientists in world history are living today and that at least half of them are working on military projects—decides to do research into the "transarmament" by which "defense industries" can be converted to civilian production. These and other similar actions will be poorly funded, precarious, and suspect. And they will contain the seeds of newness.

There are, however, three major areas in which pacifist Christians will have a distinctive contribution to make:

- *The first and most basic of these is the calling* to participate in God's new society, *the church. God's chosen means of conveying his wisdom to the principalities and powers is that of Christian faith communities (Eph. 3:10). In their common life, justice and reconciliation will be evidences of the presence of God's reign . . .*

- *A second important calling to pacifist Christians is* to be prophetic. *This is a calling that just war and pacifist Christians share . . . But there is one prophetic responsibility that is unique to pacifists. This is querying the* myth of realism *. . . It may be "realistic," but it is not reasonable, to expect anything other than conflagration to come from an arms race. Sometimes—perhaps all along—the more realistic thing to do is something "unrealistic."*

- *The third calling to pacifist Christians is* to engage in political action. *Pacifists . . . will try to persuade governments to be* more just and less violent *than they think is possible*[2] *. . . In foreign policy, they will have a special concern for reconciliation between "irreconcilable" enemies . . . In military policy, pacifists will work to encourage the consideration of less violent and nonviolent strategies in both policing and national defense. And in the areas of weaponry, pacifists will do everything they can, by means both orthodox and*

[2] John H. Yoder, *The Christian Witness to the State* (Newton, KS: Faith and Life Press, 1964), 71–73.

unorthodox (including voting, organizing, lobbying, and demon-strating), to persuade the nation to "turn its heart" about the nuclear weapons that are threatening millions of its and its enemy's people with a "sudden end" (Zeph. 1:18).[3]

....

⁚ Chris Marshall

Alan and Eleanor Kreider have been important people in my faith journey. My wife, Margaret, and I first got to know them some thirty years ago, when we visited the London Mennonite Centre in our search for a spiritual home at the beginning of our four-year sojourn in England. We had just started to learn about Anabaptism at that time, and in many ways Alan and Ellie served as living embodiments of what we were discovering, and enhanced its attractiveness immeasurably. By who they were and what they taught, they helped us to "begin to see things differently," which, as they explain in this extract, is the groundwork of Christian radicalism.

Seeing things differently—the starting point of ethics

How we see the world—that is, how we understand and interpret what is going on around us all of the time—is the starting point of ethics. The principal ethical question is not, What should I do? but, What do I believe is real? What is the world really like? Just war proponents typically commend their position as a form of realism. Pacifism, they say, is a wonderful sentiment, a truly noble aspiration. But it is unrealistic. It is impractical to think that nonviolence can actually work in the *real* world.

United States President Barack Obama made this very point in the speech he delivered on receiving the Nobel Peace Prize in December 2009. Acutely aware of the disparity that existed between

---

[3] Reprinted from Alan Kreider, "Swords into Plowshares," in *Time to Choose: A Grassroots Study Guide on the Nuclear Arms Race from a Christian Perspective*, ed. Martha Keys Barker et al. (Lytchett Minster, Dorset, England: Celebration, 1983), 76–80. Used by permission.

himself—commander in chief of the world's greatest-ever military power, locked in two major wars—and the example of nonviolent peacemaking set by Mahatma Gandhi and Martin Luther King, Obama offered a spirited defense of the just war doctrine as a necessary instrument for promoting peace in a violent world:

> I know there is nothing weak, nothing passive, nothing naive, in the creed and lives of Gandhi and King. But as a head of state sworn to protect and defend my nation, I cannot be guided by their examples alone. I face the world as it is, and cannot stand idle in the face of threats to the American people. For make no mistake: evil does exist in the world. A nonviolent movement could not have halted Hitler's armies. Negotiations cannot convince al Qaeda's leaders to lay down their arms. To say that force is sometimes necessary is not a call to cynicism—it is a recognition of history, the imperfections of man, and the limits of reason.

For Obama, to "face the world as it is," with all its existing evils, requires the use of military force. The alternative is to "stand idle in the face of threats to the American people," for nonviolence, he maintains, can never stop the Hitlers and bin Ladens and other perpetrators of mass evil. Perhaps he is right. Many would concur with him on the limitations of nonviolence, though to equate nonviolence with standing idly by and doing nothing to oppose evil is a travesty of what Gandhi and King represented.

The gospel offers an alternative to the false "myth of realism"

The point to note is that Obama, like all just warriors, counters the normativity of nonviolence by appealing to what the Kreiders call the myth of realism, the insistence that violence is the only realistic option for controlling evil. Such a belief is a myth in both senses of the word—it is a myth because it assumes a larger, and essentially pagan, narrative about the meaning and direction of cosmic history; and it is myth because its undergirding narrative, from the perspective of Christian faith, is fundamentally false.

The Christian gospel offers an alternative narrative about reality. The gospel must never be reduced to the advocacy of some ethical or political doctrine of nonviolence, even if it includes that. The gospel is, more basically, the explosive claim that a whole new world has come into being. It is the good news that the future transfiguration of reality that the biblical prophets and poets long dreamed of—a transfiguration in which the lion will lie down with the lamb and swords will be beaten into plowshares—has already begun. It has begun with the bodily resurrection of Jesus from the dead, an event that marks the definitive defeat of sin's violent tyranny over the world as we know it. This in turn means that the world as we know it is not the way the world really is.

Something has shifted in the structures of reality. A dramatic change has occurred. What John Dominic Crossan calls "God's Great Cleanup Operation" has commenced. This change may be visible at present only to the eyes of faith, but it is still absolutely real, and one day it will fill the earth as the waters cover the sea. Accordingly, as the Kreiders explain, "the pacifist Christian senses a call to participate in a new world that God is building, and to invite the old world to join in."

The call to participate in this new reality

But where does this sense of call to participate in God's new world come from, and why do so few Christians, like President Obama, manage to hear it? It comes from three places in particular.

Knowing and inhabiting the story of Jesus. First and foremost, it comes from knowing the story of Jesus, and from telling and retelling that story over and over again until we not only believe it but actually begin to inhabit it. Christian radicalism is sustainable only to the extent that it concentrates radically on the person of Jesus Christ, as the singular paradigm and empowerment of Christian peacemaking.

This is one of the things that Alan and Eleanor have taught me. Their commitment to pacifism has never come across as an ideological or political or dogmatic conviction. It has always appeared to be an expression of their love for Jesus and of their determination to follow him in life. I recall Eleanor once telling me how, as a child growing up in a Mennonite missionary family in India, the passage of scripture she was taught to know best was Matthew 5–7, the Sermon on the Mount.

How very different, I thought, from my own Christian upbringing, where favored biblical texts were those that illustrated the "four spiritual laws" and that invited the baptism of the Holy Spirit. In my church background, the ethical teaching of Jesus, or for that matter the overarching story of Jesus' earthly career, was rarely discussed and only considered paradigmatic when it came to praying for miracles! No wonder I imbibed little sense that the Christian faith is all about participating in a new world and cultivating new practices and priorities, including peacemaking, befitting that world.

Belonging to the church, God's new society. The second place where an awareness of the call to belong to a new world springs is from belonging to the church, or being part of God's new society, as the Kreiders call it. Admittedly the church doesn't often look all that new or different from the world around it. It's not hard, and in some circles is quite fashionable, to feel deeply cynical about the church. But we ought to resist such cynicism. Certainly the empirical churches most of us know fall far short of the radical faith communities of love and justice we read of in the New Testament. But this discrepancy should occasion no surprise and is no cause for despair. For, as the apostle Paul reminds us, "we have this treasure in jars of clay to show that this all-surpassing power is from God and not from us" (2 Cor. 4:7; NIV).

The clay jar that is the church looks pretty much like any other clay jar on the shelf. But within this jar, as roughly cast and fragile as it is, there lies an extraordinary power that comes from God, a power that shines as light in the darkness and overcomes death with the promise of life, a power that gives hope in the face of violence and oppression. "We are hard pressed on every side, but not crushed; perplexed, but not in despair; persecuted, but not abandoned; struck down, but not destroyed" (2 Cor. 4:8–9; NIV).

What is this all-surpassing power that Paul speaks of? It is the power of the gospel story the church treasures, the story of

Jesus' life, death, and resurrection and the outpouring of the Spirit. And it is this empowering story, and only this story, that makes the church different from any other group in society. As Stanley Hauerwas observes, the church is unique not because of its superior morality or piety or aesthetic sensibilities but because it is the only community on earth that gathers around the true story.

The church is God's new society not because it is perfect but because it is the only society that has been formed by the story of the new world God has brought about through Jesus Christ. It is utterly disastrous, history teaches, when the church forgets or neglects or distorts or betrays its formative story. But without the church the story would be lost forever, and it is only by belonging to the church that our sense of being called to participate in God's new world can be kept alive.

Participating in Christian activism and protest. The third way it is kept alive is through Christian activism and prophetic protest. Here the Kreiders are especially helpful, and totally realistic. They recognize that the immediate consequences of embracing nonviolent peacemaking are unknowable. Sometimes a pacifist response will succeed in frustrating evildoers and in transforming enemies into friends. At other times it will not. Sometimes God will work miracles of deliverance and provision. At other times God will not, and there will be suffering and a cross.

The results are unpredictable and will often be costly. But that does not alter the nature of the call. For Christians are not called to straighten out the world through their own energetic efforts. They are called, rather, to bear witness in their words and deeds to God's work of straightening out the world through Jesus Christ, and to do so in a manner that is compatible with God's nonviolent way of working.

This means that Christian pacifists must be selective in the jobs they do, the professions they pursue, the tasks they take on within their careers. There is nothing wrong with being selective, though pacifists are often accused of an unacceptable form of dualism at this point. But all people are selective in their vocations to a significant degree. To be selective is not to withdraw from the world; it is to engage with the world in a particular way. It is also to engage with the world in a realistic way, for what one considers realistic or reasonable depends, finally, on what one thinks is real, how one construes the deepest meaning of reality.

In any event, the pacifist witness must be an activist witness. It can never be, as Obama implies, a case of standing idly by and doing nothing in face of evil. Instead, in the Kreiders' words, it is a matter of "doing positive and distinctive things that will bring in the newness of God's kingdom."

I am immensely grateful for Alan's and Eleanor's influence in my life. Their humility, gentleness, goodness, and Christian learning have been a beacon for me in my own life and work over the past three decades. I only hope that in some small way I have been able to pass on to others some of what I have learned from them, and I continue to aspire to display the qualities of character I have observed in them.

⋮ Simon Barrow

In psychosomatic terms, temporal distance is liable to degrade, distort, and cloud the memory—or else to enhance it in stimulating but equally questionable ways! However, in spiritual terms, provided that realistic account is taken of our fallibilities, that same distance can become graced space in which perspective is gained, wounds are contextualized, and deep thankfulness is realized.

This is what comes to me as I reflect on my own connections with Alan and Eleanor, as I read Chris Marshall's clear-sighted rooting of their Christian pacifism in the world redescribed through Christ, and as I call to mind the gifts that Alan, the theologically inspired historian, and Ellie, the theologically inspired liturgist, have shared so widely over the years. What I mean by *theology* in these settings—ones they have blessed—is wrestling with the unfathomable mystery of God, but to enlighten rather than to obscure.

I first met the Kreiders as an enthusiastic young Christian in the late 1970s. At the time I was moved by the biblical message of hope for the world, immersed in the troubled politics of my generation, and seeking congruence between these two, which I struggled to discover in the faith patterns of my inherited church. Lurching between a Christian social activism that could be thin on spiritual resources, and a Christendom-shaped quietism that was ill equipped to question worldly realism, I began to find through them fresh resources—ones for understanding how the calling of the eternal could be responded to faithfully and critically within the constraints of the temporal.

Active peacemaking as the gospel's means of affirming the alternative realism made available in the cross and resurrection—*that* would be my core understanding of what those resources look like today. Chris Marshall traces the theological, missiological, Christological, and ecclesiological contours of intentional Christian nonviolence (I find the word *pacifism* inadequate) with an elegant, knowing simplicity that is reflective of Alan and Eleanor's style too. Their charism lies in being able to condense disciplined learning and tough prayer—those two inseparable components of Christianly formed habits of mind—into messages for the church, and through it the world, which are inspiring, communicable, and enlivening.

In my work with Ekklesia[+] I am sometimes asked questions like these: What is your theory of the state? What is your theology of the media? I find myself saying things that go right back to an incidental remark Alan once made to me in his study at the London Mennonite Centre, around 1978. I cannot quite recall what it was (a junior moment swallowed up in a senior one, perhaps!), but it enabled me to realize for the first time that what I really needed was an ecclesiology—an account of the Christian community and my vocation within it. Not in order to out-theorize others or to set myself above them, but as a way of discerning, with others, the voice of Christ amid storms of complexity. *Deo gracias.*

[+] See www.ekklesia.co.uk.

⦂ Cathy Nobles

From the beginning of the Reconciliation Walk, as I prepared to train Christian teams coming from the West to apologize for the Crusades, I would often ask myself: how did the church progress from a gospel in which Jesus taught his disciples to love their enemies, to a movement that killed under the sign of the cross? I knew bits of this story, but until I heard Alan's teaching and saw Alan and Ellie's faith in action, I did not fully grasp the depth of the transformation needed to walk as a peacemaker.

Alan taught on the Reconciliation Walk in Cappadocia, Turkey, in 1997. I was fascinated, and so were the walk participants. As Alan drew from the writings of the early church their way of living out Jesus' teachings, we began to glimpse the depth of attitudinal change that enabled Christians to love their enemies and make peace with one another. His study of the early church's transformation under Constantine to Christendom, and its merging of the power of state and church, was the bridge I needed to interpret the Crusades and to see why we need to transform this historical legacy.

The values Alan taught have challenged me and others to live differently. On the Reconciliation Walk, when we met Turks, Syrians, Lebanese, Israelis, and Palestinians (whether they were Jewish, Muslim, or Christian), we apologized with a new humility. In our orientations, the mainly Western teams, confronted with the violence of the Crusades and the damage they did to our gospel witness, repented of feeling superior to other faiths or nations and began to catch a glimpse of the road of humility we are called to walk with others. In laying down our weapons of war, including a sense of cultural superiority or nationalism, teams began to be more sensitive to the Holy Spirit and his leadings.

For many of us, the idea that living in peace with one another is possible and important to our witness was a wake-up call. Our teams were taught to make peace with one another as the early Christians had done, so that others would see the gospel lived out in community. Often teams were asked how people from different backgrounds could live and travel together in peace, and what had drawn them together to this project. Here were the echoes of what Alan taught us about how the church is called to wage peace among ourselves and with our neighbors, and that when we do this others are interested in our witness.

In coming with repentant hearts, we began to listen to the stories of pain along the Crusade route with less nationalistic defensiveness. We had more sympathy for people who have often felt vilified by history and today's media. And we began to see how it is possible to love your "enemy" and become friends with people from various faiths and nations.

Alan encouraged us to be people that others want to gossip about, as the Romans did about the early church, because God's love is a way of peace that opens doors for others to be loved by our Father. Alan and Ellie's influence in my life and the lives of all who led and participated in the Reconciliation Walk will stand as testimony of God making a way for a new generation to begin to learn how to live in peace in a conflicted age.

7

Anabaptism
Follow in Jesus' footsteps

Anabaptism Today? *This may sound somewhat immodest. Anabaptism, in its generative and expansive form at least, was crushed more than four centuries ago. The established churches, often for understandable reasons of responsibility and institutional survival, rejected its insights. Its leaders were killed or cowed into quiescence. Its writings remained unpublished and unread. The very word* Anabaptism *became a byword for fanaticism and tumult.*

Beginning about a century ago, however, and gaining momentum in the past twenty years, there has been a growing readiness on the part of many Christians to listen to the Anabaptists. There is new interest in listening not only to the Anabaptists but also to marginal Christians from other times and places who had parallel insights. At a time when Christianity manifestly is in trouble, at least in the Northern Hemisphere, a growing number of Christians are turning to unexpected sources for ways forward.

Christians are turning to the past not out of nostalgia but to reawaken subversive memories. Things have been and can be other than as they are. There is no God-given inevitability about forms of Christian witness and church life that past generations have bequeathed to us. God's Spirit, who reminds us of everything Jesus taught (John 14:26), also reminds us of undomesticated forms of Christian living. Though crushed and marginalized in the past, in our time these can address us with new possibilities for thought, action, and common life. Anabaptism's new influence today is an expression of this. It indicates the transforming potential of a repressed memory brought back into consciousness . . .

Voluntarist, nonconformist, communitarian, Christocentric—these themes emerge from Anabaptist writings and court records that scholars have uncovered in recent decades. The Anabaptists, whose memory was persecuted by powerful people who write histories, now for the first time in almost five centuries have been able to speak for themselves . . . Some, in hot disagreement, will point out "That's an Anabaptist *argument!" But this put-down doesn't work as well as it used to. Less and less can people categorize an alternative point of view as Anabaptist and think that they have thereby dismissed it. An increasing number of Christians, finding that traditional Christian formulations and folkways no longer fit the world in which they live, are discovering intriguing relevance in the Anabaptists' word and way.*[1]

....

⋮ Erin Dufault Hunter

At the interdenominational evangelical seminary in which I teach, adherents to Anabaptist traditions—as well as overt sympathizers—have recently increased not only in number but also in influence. In some cases they have chairs or senior level positions. On one occasion a faculty colleague commented openly on this development, half serious in his concern about the undue influence such a minority perspective was having on the community. But a high-level administrator quickly retorted, "Oh, don't worry. That's the thing with Anabaptists—actually *give* them power, and they don't know what to do with it."

This joke works because it plays on the truth of Anabaptist experience from a number of angles. It reminds us of our past, as those who have been on the underside of Christian history, seemingly tangential to the story of the church. It notes the shifting sands of favor, as Anabaptism's marginalization has ironically prepared

---

[1] Reprinted from Alan Kreider, "The Search for Roots," *Anabaptism Today* 1 (November 1992): 5–7. Used by permission of the publisher.

it for a prophetic role in postmodern, post-Christendom culture. The worried colleague and the sharp administrator both assume that Anabaptism threatens the powers that be, upends the status quo. The clever retort reminds us that the most cunning among the powerful know that an effective way of squelching disruptive movements is to offer them their own place among the honored, even by officially recognizing them as resident radicals. The shift from subversive to submissive can be surprisingly subtle.

The temptations of influence

Anabaptism's attraction affords us a unique opportunity to influence the church in ways we had only dreamed about. But popularity—or what I dub the "coolness" factor of Anabaptism among my students—contains its own temptations. Undisciplined by particular habits of heart and mind, Anabaptism too quickly becomes like those it seeks to challenge. No longer a source of renewal and hope, no longer a witness to the possibilities of God in the ordinary, we risk becoming enamored of our identity as subversives, as the truly radical, as the extraordinary. Once we laud ourselves as such, we have betrayed the Lamb and played by the rules of the lion.

If subversion or "radicalness" becomes the end of Anabaptist faith, we have lost our witness to Christ, who provides the contours of our life, and instead we identify ourselves not by our allegiance to the way of Jesus but over against the way things are. In the end, such a move disembowels us, forcing us to speak a language not of scripture but of upheaval, missing the distinctly Christocentric message that transforms mere resistance into prophetic engagement. We must remind ourselves that our subversiveness finds its life-giving shape from within the gospel story. Apart from Christ, it serves other gods and other goods.

If Anabaptism is to fulfill its potential influence in the present age, we need to attend to our identity as *Ana*-baptists—as those whose lives are marked by repeated submersion into the life of Christ, who in his own baptism subverted expectations about why messiahs are anointed and how they exhibit greatness. In his submission to God in his baptism by John, Jesus identified with the ones he came to save, with his enemies, with those who rejected him. Following the baptized Christ, we must habituate ourselves to humble subversion characterized by an undomesticated fire—a fire born not of reactionary fervor but of the Spirit.

Habituated into humble subversion

By remembering the ways of Christ and of our own tradition, we do not so much seek to undermine what exists but endeavor to *turn* it, to encourage repentance as Jesus does after his baptism. In my field of ethics, work dominating the academy often claims to be subversive. Seeking to support the oppressed, these ethicists unmask the ways the mighty claim to attend to universal or shared interests yet do so in order to distract from their own voracious appetite for power and incessant seeking of their own benefit. As Samuel Wells notes, "By articulating the suppressed voices, subversive ethics challenges those in power to demonstrate whether they have any authority beyond the implicit threat of violence."[2]

Unfortunately, such ethics too seldom turns enemies into friends; it does battle against the powerful but offers little hope for reconciliation. And once the oppressed gain advantage, they too frequently adopt the patterns and power plays of those they overthrew. Such ethics is more aptly named rebellion, not subversion. Although purporting to speak for the marginalized, it has become a dominant strain of conversation, even among comfortably middle-class academics.

This paradox serves as a warning to Anabaptists, who articulate repressed memories and alternative interpretations of the church's story. One way to keep the potentially disruptive from becoming truly dangerous is to allow us a space for our protests. Thus domesticated, we speak freely and hear the pleasing echo of our assured, righteous tones. Such tamed subversives disrupt little and turn few. Anabaptists must resist being penned up in this way, limited to one stratum of church or society, acquiescing in identification with the "progressive" or "socially active."

---

[2] See Samuel Wells, *God's Companions: Reimagining Christian Ethics* (Oxford: Blackwell, 2006), 4.

Co-option of the Anabaptist vision can take place in multiple ways and in various guises. For example, our peacemaking expertise has become well regarded; people, organizations, even nations seek our help in building consensus and developing harmonious societies, families, and institutions. This acceptance honors the diligence of those who honed the skills and habits needed to wage peace; this work remains a crucial ministry to our world that witnesses to what is possible when humans cooperate with God's good grace. It is this ministry of reconciliation through nonviolence, so crucial to the New Testament understanding of the church's calling, that has attracted many to the gospel for the first time and brought others back to it with renewed vigor.

Yet the temptation remains to become identified in this work not by the One into whom we were baptized but by human companionships, concerns, and values. We might easily be flattered and adopt the labels offered us, without realizing that doing so quarantines our message. To accept such branding is to be marketed as a small and endearing slice of Christian history, agitators who ultimately remain minor-league idealists who support those of real influence and acumen.

We are subversive, but subversive in a uniquely Christian, "baptized" way, as those who accept the power offered us by the Spirit through the disciplines of humble service and identification with our ever-shifting enemies. Jesus' baptism anointed him as Messiah, as the one on whom salvation depended, who would indeed turn the world back to shalom. Yet the positional tactics of this king—out in the desert, among the poor, with those who will reject him— remind us of our own baptismal promises to do the same. If we forget our baptism, we forget that we too are the enemies for whom Christ descended into the depths of death and hell. We become, like rebels everywhere, lulled by the sound of our own self-righteous voices into mirroring dominant approaches to influence or illusions of greatness.

Partnerships for renewal

At some points in our history, we have acquiesced to being the "quiet in the land," to not having power, as if ceding strength to the mighty was itself the virtue of humility. But that quietism is not the best of Anabaptism, which from in its inception proclaimed and lived the truth that transformation comes from below, that it is the meek who finally inherit the earth.

Our model is Christ himself. Our source of sustenance is the Spirit who deigns to dwell among us. As Christ humbly identified with those lost to the world's ways and captive to its lies, we too must acknowledge that we share more than we like to admit with our detractors—particularly those who resist our re-membering of the Christian story and resent our growing influence.

To use our newfound attractiveness in ways unlike the way of the baptized Messiah is our temptation. We are tempted to bask in the attention but fail to use it to underscore our mutual need for grace and our shared dependence on God for effecting shalom. Just as there was no virtue in refusing the responsibility of influence, there is also no virtue in identifying as those who most truly comprehend Christ or as rebels in the land. Instead, like Christ, we eat with our enemies, including those in the Christian family who most resist our pressure to renew faith by attending to forgotten alternative readings of our common story.

In my context, this necessitates lively conversation—and occasionally impassioned argument—with denominational traditions and strands of the church that have persecuted my adopted Anabaptist tradition, who have written the histories in which we are caricatured. Despite deep and abiding differences, we share in the baptism of Christ, and that provides hope that we can humbly cooperate with the Spirit and with one another to forge a new, unexpected way forward for the missio Dei today. Alan and Eleanor Kreider's work and writings display this sensibility; they have acted as humble subversives, making friends across Europe while holding fast to Anabaptist particularities that beckon others to turn to God in Christ.

The story in the beginning of this chapter reminds us of what is actually occurring: we are being challenged to contribute to the body, or in the playful rejoinder above, are being tested to see whether we can deliver as effective leaders if afforded the opportunity. The question has never been whether Christians can have power, though this has been the mistaken impression of some Anabaptists who failed to attend to the ways Christ's own baptism presses us to enact true greatness.

The question is rather, in what does lasting significance consist and how do we achieve it? Like Christ in the desert, we must resist temptations to adopt various and subtle invitations to power from above. We cannot identify as rebels who heckle the world's powers but effect little change. We cannot self-righteously gloat as outsiders who revel in the failure of other Christians' tactics. Instead we actively turn the world toward God by emerging again and again from baptismal waters, repenting of our own bent intentions yet simultaneously strengthened for the good work the gospel affords us in this exciting age.

Some are offering authority to us, placing their trust in our collective wisdom and memory as an important resource for the church's mission today. Often from unimportant subterranean spaces, Anabaptists challenge the givens of Christendom and provide a counterpoint to narratives of both realists and romantics—the realists whose imaginations are stunted by acute awareness of sin, and the romantics who believe new life can come without sharing in others' weakness or acknowledging their own.

If we consistently reenter the waters of forgiveness for living as disaffected rebels or as complacently pious Christians, then Anabaptism will emerge as a faithful witness to God's uncontainable creativity and surprising grace. We can surface from below empowered by the Spirit and accompanied by unexpected friends. Together we will seek the good of a North American society littered by staid Christian institutions and old forms of faith that long for renewal by means of those same waters, by that same Spirit.

⋮ **Moriah Hurst**

I have grown up with one foot in North America and the other on the east coast of Australia. My parents have worked for one or another Mennonite organization for most of my life, and while I have studied at three Mennonite institutions, I have spent a significant part of my life in places where Anabaptism is mostly unknown.

Growing up in Australia—a country that knows next to nothing about Anabaptism—has meant that from the age of nine, I have had to articulate what Anabaptism is to people who wondered if I was describing a cult. Australians see just being part of a church as strange enough. Add to that that I am a member of a weird sect with origins requiring me to take people back nearly five hundred years in order to explain its identity, and with affiliations to the Amish who can on occasion serve as a point of reference or conversation starter, yet whose reality fails to capture Anabaptism in the way I want to describe or present it. In short, owning Anabaptism has been a bit odd, but maybe that's just the point. I grew up knowing that we need to be in the world but not of it, so being odd is good.

Today I work with youth and young adults in Australia's capital city. Far too often the faith I see young people being given is little more than a list of don'ts—don't drink, don't smoke, and don't sleep around. In Australian culture, refusing to do these things does make you odd. But I believe that our faith, particularly in the Anabaptist tradition, calls us on to something more.

I want to be part of calling young people *to* something, not just *away* from things: calling them to a faith in which Jesus is central, a faith that isn't just about "the good life" with a Sunday morning outing. As Anabaptists we try to read the Bible in community and ask questions about how this reading informs the ins and outs of our daily life. We read the Gospels and look at how Jesus lived and what he taught, seeing this life, these teachings, as a guide for our lives, not a handbook of religious rules and regulations for fanatics.

Anabaptism is still relatively unknown and rather odd here in Australia, though more people are familiar with the name than was the case twenty years ago. My parents decided early on not to plant a Mennonite church in Australia. This country already has many denominations and doesn't really need another one. Yet Anabaptism still has much to offer to other Christian traditions. A participatory, nonviolent, active, Bible-immersed, Jesus-centered faith is needed here as much as it is in Goshen, Indiana, in Switzerland, or in Germany. This old tradition is a new thing here, breathing fresh life into dusty religious corners.

⁝ Tim Foley

One enduring memory I have of Alan and Ellie's ministry is their teaching among the study groups of the United Kingdom Anabaptist Network. They would arrive with copies of some early Anabaptist source, heavily underlined in places, and the group, representing people from all across the church spectrum, would dialogue with the original thoughts of Balthasar Hubmaier or Pilgram Marpeck. This approach proved to be an invigorating way to encounter the thought and energy of the early Anabaptists.

I remember thanking Alan for underlining what I took to be the important parts of Hubmaier, and he somewhat sternly responded, "The underlining does not mean that I agree with it!" (I think he wanted me to work harder.) Looking through the Kreiders' published works I don't see much directly written on the early Anabaptists. Others were doing this work, so Alan and Ellie were free to write on contemporary missional topics such as worship, peace church, holiness, and the early church, yet always through Anabaptist lenses.

Given their gifts, I sometimes wondered whether it was a sacrifice for them to give so much energy to the grassroots rather than the academic. They could have taken more secure and more prominent academic posts, but instead they chose to be mission workers. They discerned that the UK setting required translation and application of Anabaptist convictions for a people who had no family connection to Mennonites, who were more likely to be Anglican, Baptist, or New Church, but were searching for a home. This reality would later become known as "hyphenated Anabaptism."

I like this strategy and was one of the beneficiaries of it! It is a good illustration of Erin Dufault Hunter's point about the Kreiders as "humble subversives, making friends across Europe while holding fast to Anabaptist particularities that beckon others to turn to God in Christ."

This is a tough line to walk, respecting and affirming other Christian traditions while holding fast to Anabaptist particularities. Alan and Ellie did it well and saved some of us from a narrow, superior, and exclusive understanding of Anabaptism. None of us has arrived; we are all on the journey toward Christ. They taught us that the integrity of our witness depends on the world noticing our love for one another—a point their friend Walter Sawatsky regularly highlights as one of the great mission challenges. They helped us have a more generous orthodoxy.

But it was more than a mission strategy. They seem to be genuinely attracted to other expressions of the Christian faith. I remember stories they told of retreats in a Catholic liturgical setting and of their friendships with monks and bishops. I can't resist mentioning Brother Eoin de Bhaldraithe from Bolton Abbey, Kildare—dairy farmer, scholar of Celtic Christianity, and Anabaptist. A few years ago he told me that he was, like me, using the Sermon on the Mount for his devotional reading. Our approaches were a little different— several months into the year he was still on the Beatitudes! Yet . . . Anabaptists and Catholics learning from each other? The Kreiders would have it so.

III.
Community

8

Catechesis and baptism
Learn to be disciples

In baptism, Christ sets us free from the power of sin. The particular shape of sin varies with each potential Christian. Catechesis isn't a quick thing; in its classical form, it's a journey toward baptism. It is an interactive time, in which relationships are built and candidates are enabled to experience change, to own, understand, and confess their bondages—and then they are brought to Christ who can set them free. It is a time of learning, but learning that happens as much by practice as by study. It is a time of formation, as Christ is formed in them and as their reflexes are re-reflexed to be Christ-like. The early North African theologian Tertullian understood this. He said, "Christians are not born but made."[1]

But the process of making Christians cannot be quick. According to the Apostolic Tradition, *a third-century church order, "Catechumens shall continue to hear the word for three years."*[2] *Of course, just because some early churches did something is no reason that twenty-first-century Christians should do it. "Deep church" doesn't mean "patristic fundamentalism."*[3]

---

[1] Tertullian, *Apology* 18.

[2] *Apostolic Tradition* 17. Maxwell E. Johnson (*The Rites of Christian Initiation: Their Evolution and Interpretation* [Collegeville, MN: Liturgical Press, 1999], 91) doubts that anything as long as a three-year catechumenate was normal practice prior to the fourth century; various bits of evidence lead me to disagree—I think of the catechetical work of Origen in Caesarea, which presupposed an extensive period of catechesis, or of the eleventh canon of the early fourth-century synod of Elvira which had provision for a five-year catechumenate.

[3] I first encountered this provocative term in Joan M. Peterson, "House-Churches in Rome," *Vigiliae Christianae* 23, no. 4 (1969): 264.

But I insist. As we prepare candidates for baptism today, let the prepa-rations last not six weeks but sixty weeks, or even ninety weeks, which is only half of what the Apostolic Tradition *specifies. These are of course round numbers. When I ask a Catholic friend of mine, who is active in catechesis, "How long should catechesis last?" he answers, "As long as it takes." It can be shorter, depending on the candidate—but it can last a year and a half, as it does in some congregations today, or longer. And baptismal preparations should involve not only the baptismal candidate but also the candidate's mentor or sponsor, and if possible, a group of bap-tismal pilgrims, traveling together toward initiation. Baptismal prepara-tion is done in relationship!*

But why should baptismal preparations take so long? Think for a moment about the culture that surrounds us. Think how advertising catechizes us. Think of the peer pressure in our social, school, and work environments. Think of the reflex-shaping power of television, the Internet, and video games. An English youth from a Christian home may have gone to Sunday school; he may have attended a Crusaders Group.[+] *By age eighteen he may have been in Sunday school and Crusaders for 750 hours. But he will have spent 11,000 hours in school and 15,000 hours watching television. In these circumstances, where is catechesis really happening? What chance does the church have of shaping its young people—their convictions and identities, their ambitions and drives, their ideas of what it is to be successful and fulfilled?*

Another statistic that illustrates the problem: in 2002 the United States advertising industry, whose business is evangelizing us, spent $237 billion. How much in comparison did the church spend in shaping the views and longings of its members? The advertisers are experts; they prey without ceasing on our insecurities and desires. If the church is to evaluate the spiritual realities that evangelize us, and if the church is to enable Christians to live creatively in the midst of these realities, it has got to ask: what kinds of teaching, what alternative means of socialization, can the churches use to form people who want to be Christians? "I am in the pains of childbirth," says Paul, "until Christ is formed in you" (Gal. 4:19). We don't want to baptize Christo-pagans. We don't want to allow the world

---

[+] [A Christian youth organization, now happily renamed "Urban Saints."—Ed.]

to squeeze us into its mold. So what forms of catechetical formation can we use?

I believe that a journey of baptismal preparation—catechesis—that culminates in baptism is the best type of formation that we've got. The journey should be relatively leisurely. It trains people to think and live as Christians, and it looks forward to baptism as a time of joyful arrival. So, the church will not baptize people because they grew up in Christian families or because they have a good conversion story. It will not baptize them because they are nice, or hardworking, or conforming, or pleasing to parents, peers, or neighbors.

But the church will baptize people who have taken part in a journey with others and have demonstrated that they are willing to say "Jesus is Lord" and mean it. The church will baptize those who have come to know Jesus and are willing to think and live as his disciples, those who have taken part in a process in which they have learned to understand their culture, the problems and opportunities that postmodernity and post-Christendom present to disciples of Jesus.

In this process they have learned about themselves—what their besetting sins are. They have learned what the gospel is—that God in Christ has graciously forgiven them, and is setting them free, liberating them from addictions, filling them with the power of the Holy Spirit to be disciples of Jesus and to participate in God's mission in a world in which it is hard to be Christian but which God loves passionately. On this journey culminating in baptism they have come to a watershed. From now on, they, incorporate "in Christ," will be walking as Jesus people![5]

....

[5] Reprinted from Alan Kreider, "Baptism and Catechesis as Spiritual Formation," in *Remembering Our Future: Explorations in Deep Church*, ed. Andrew Walker and Luke Bretherton (Milton Keynes, Buckinghamshire, England: Paternoster Press, 2007), 170–206, Used by permission.

⦂ Ian Stackhouse

I had the privilege of hearing Alan deliver the paper from which this extract is taken at a Deep Church Conference here at Guildford Baptist Church, Millmead, back in 2007.[6] Those of us who were present for the various papers all agreed that it was the outstanding contribution of the two-day event. In part this was because of Alan's winsome personality. In so many ways Alan embodies the virtues he is seeking to celebrate in his writings.

But the impact of his paper was a result of the fact that he highlighted what must be the biggest challenge the church faces in our increasingly secular and decadent culture—the ancient but urgent task of catechesis. Preaching is one thing; it has its own place in the panoply of ministry the church must deploy. But all great preaching—as indeed all great worship—relies on the presence of a catechized congregation in order for it to be effective.

In recalling the paper that Alan delivered, I have to confess that there was some bewilderment immediately afterward. Since many of the pastors who were present that day had no doubt preached their way through the book of Acts at some time, our initial reaction to the prospect of "not six weeks but sixty weeks, or even ninety weeks" of catechesis *prior* to baptism was fairly negative. Ethiopian eunuchs come to mind at this point. Indeed, I hardly dare admit this to Alan, but just a few days after the conference we had one of those spontaneous moments in our church, with someone rushing forward at the end of one of our planned baptisms asking to be immersed in water there and then. On briefly questioning her, I had no good reason to hinder her.

Long-term catechesis—essential, vital, and integral to spiritual formation

But that confession aside at long last, I want to affirm that we all resonated with the burden of Alan's paper, namely, that long-term catechesis must become a vital and integral part of our spiritual for-

---

[6] See n5 above.

mation. If we think that three-week courses here, or a few sermons there, are sufficient for the work of orienting new believers to the strange new world of the scriptures, then we are badly mistaken. As Robert Jenson states with reference to the emergence of prebaptismal catechesis in the strikingly similar context of ancient paganism, "life in the church was just too different from life out of the church for people to tolerate the transfer without some preparation."[7]

My own recent forays into catechetical work with new believers who are devoid of any childhood upbringing in the church confirms what Alan argues here—that it is impossible to underestimate the time needed to thoroughly "detox" a person from the prevailing values of an increasingly neopagan culture and immerse them into the values of the kingdom of God.

In retrospect, I guess this kind of experience is why Alan would argue that instruction ought to take place prior to baptism—something that three years on from the conference I am increasingly coming to see and understand. The fact of the matter is that we are not in the same situation as those earliest converts in the book of Acts. Back to our Ethiopian eunuch: when was the last time we sat next to a person on a bus who was reading from the scroll of the prophet Isaiah? More likely such people will be reading *The Prophet*, by Khalil Gibran. The people turning up in our churches now are two to three generations away from the teaching ministry of the church. Even after one year with my first group of catechumens back in 2007, I felt that I was only just beginning to get to the real issues facing a group coming from a culture where there is a deep hostility to dogma and where ethical discernment has become tantamount in certain instances to deciding whether something is fun or boring.[8]

---

[7] R. W. Jenson, "Catechesis for Our Time," in *Marks of the Body of Christ*, ed. Carl Braaten and R. W. Jenson (Grand Rapids, MI: Eerdmans, 1999), 137–49.

[8] See Neil Postman, *Amusing Ourselves to Death: Public Discourse in the Age of Show Business* (London: Methuen, 1985).

Catechism should seek to transform both belief and behavior

Indeed, the experience of working with a group of catechumens for whom consumer choice is the dominant creed—as it is in our churches, of course—has confirmed for me that the real challenge of what Alan brings to us from his Anabaptist tradition is this: if we are serious about initiation, it is not enough to think in terms of doctrinal formulations, important as these are; we must also to think in terms of ethics. After all, the focus of training for new believers preparing for baptism, as Alan writes elsewhere, lay not just in the area of creeds but also in the area of lifestyle.[9] It is not so much confession or decision of faith but the obedience of the faith that is important, as Paul emphasizes in the opening chapters of Romans.

Coming from the Reformed tradition, I find this a challenge. I am aware of how easy it is to deliver a body of teaching and assume not only that it has been understood but also that it will translate into changed behavior. But if catechesis is to prove effective as a means of initiating new believers into the way of the kingdom of God, then it must combine doctrine with ethics—even as it must root its ethics in worship.[10]

As Roy Searle, founder of the Northumbria Community, said on an Advent retreat day at Millmead in 2009, those of us involved in the teaching ministry of the church might be better employed running courses for new believers on anger management than on three different views of the atonement, since it is here in the area of conflict that Christian discipleship so often flounders.[11] Furthermore, if we are to be true to the Jesus tradition we must ask our baptismal candidates as many pertinent questions about money and wealth as we do about the creeds, for it is here that the real battles

---

[9] Alan Kreider, *The Change of Conversion and the Origin of Christendom* (Harrisburg, PA: Trinity Press, 1999), 21–32.

[10] Stanley Hauerwas and William Willimon, *The Truth about God: The Ten Commandments in the Christian Life* (Nashville, TN: Abingdon Press, 1999), 16–23.

[11] See Dallas Willard, *The Divine Conspiracy: Rediscovering Our Hidden Life in God* (London: Fount, 1998), 43–70.

with the dominant culture take place. As one observer humorously put it, one's wallet is often the last thing to get converted. Any catechetical program that skirts this issue isn't being true to the prophetic nature of New Testament discipleship.

In which case, as Alan so rightly points out, this catechetical process involves not simply study but practice. As with Alcoholics Anonymous, the success of any good detox program is the effectiveness of the sponsors who take the material we have learned and make time to journey with us in the nitty-gritty of actual life. Otherwise, all we will have is a file of notes but no discernible transformation in the life of the believer.

Spiritual formation will fail without companions along the way

In fact, as I look back on the many commitment courses we have run over the years, and the many baptismal classes that we have advertised, it seems to me that this is the one glaring deficiency in what we do: we run a course, teach a doctrine, and even baptize a believer, and then we are surprised when we never see them again. Why? The answer is obvious. Discipleship requires companions along the way, just as it requires a community who will stay with us long enough for something to truly form. As Brett Webb-Mitchell so rightly adduces, "Being in the church is itself a catechesis because the church is constantly forming and nurturing us in God's love."[12] It is a matter not of simply running a few courses but of immersion in the life of the Christian community—its worship, its liturgy, and its communitarian life—in order that we might be shaped by it.

In the fast-paced world of the southeast of England, this kind of intentionality is problematic. Leisureliness of the kind Alan advocates, whereby we allow the ordinary life of a Christian community to shape us, is not something our churches value a great deal. Nor do we value the long-term stability required for real spiritual formation. The way people shop around for the "right" church indi-

---

[12] Brett Webb-Mitchell, *Christly Gestures: Learning to be Members of the Body of Christ* (Grand Rapids, MI: Eerdmans, 2003), 166.

cates that long-term fidelity to a community is more the exception than the rule.

Doing church has overtaken the less sensational task of being the church, and most tragic of all, pastors collude in focusing on numerical growth of the church rather than on fostering the qualitative spiritual life of the church. Until this problem with priorities is addressed, I see little hope for the kind of church renewal Alan envisages. What we can do, however, is take some steps in the right direction, trusting that all great renewals in the life of the church start with a remnant.

Doing theology—by initiating new believers into the ways of the God's kingdom

In fact it was on that basis that a few years ago we embarked on a program of catechesis in our church, or at least the semblance of one. This program is doubtless not as rigorous as Alan would have it, but I am sure he would agree that it is going in the right direction. As someone who has sought to align himself in a somewhat modest way to the pastor-scholar tradition, I find it a natural thing to be doing. After all, as someone pointed out to me, all the early church fathers were first and foremost catechists.

It is obvious when you think about it. Early church leaders did their theology in the context of the ekklesia—in particular, in the context of initiating new believers into the ways of the kingdom. The idea that you can do theology in detachment from this context, as so often happens in scholastic theology, just didn't occur to them. Their best energies were employed in establishing new believers in the faith.[13]

As someone who had chosen to work out his theology in the context of the church rather than the academy, I found this reminder was all the incentive I needed to begin. Three years on, I have learned that it is a lot more challenging than I had thought, but I am discovering, even so, what Alan has known for a long time: that there is nothing more exhilarating. And if we are worried that our

---

[13] In fact, one could make a good argument that much of the New Testament was framed in this context.

churches will diminish in numbers as a result of raising the bar, let us remember what Alan concludes from the first three centuries of very intensive catechesis: that the early church grew in accordance with the disincentive to join it.

⋮ Andy Brubacher Kaethler

The call for extensive catechesis in Alan Kreider's essay and Ian Stackhouse's response is compelling. One practical implication of this call is that we also need to account for ways contemporary Western culture is incommensurate with the missio Dei and thus why practices of resistance need to be included among the practices Kreider advocates.

One might respond to the call to extensive catechesis today with the same heaviness and sadness that consumed the rich young man Jesus encountered, who was not prepared to bear the weight of discipleship because it meant a new way of life (Mark 10:17–24). Whether the reason for such sadness is lack of imagination, lack of hope, fear of change, or being comfortable being comfortable, most of us are not prepared to resist the allures of Western culture. In truth, we are disciples of Western culture first, and disciples of Jesus only to the degree that following Jesus does not require us to question basic Western cultural values.

What characterizes Western cultural values? Some claim the prominent feature of Western culture is technology.[14] A study from 2005 reveals the faith most Christian adults in the United States pass to their youth is best characterized as "moralistic therapeutic deism."[15] To these descriptors Walter Brueggemann adds militarism and consumerism.[16] Together, technology, consumerism, militarism, moralism, therapeutism, and deism function as a web of

---

[14] Albert Borgmann, *Technology and the Character of Contemporary Life: A Philosophical Inquiry* (Chicago: University of Chicago Press, 1984).

[15] Christian Smith and Melinda Lundquist Denton, *Soul Searching: The Religious and Spiritual Lives of American Teenagers* (New York: Oxford University Press, 2005).

[16] Walter Brueggemann, "Counterscript: Living with the Elusive God," *Christian Century* 122, no. 24 (November 29, 2005), 22–28.

influences, but neither in isolation nor collectively do they reflect the story of the life of Jesus or the missio Dei.

One response is *anamnesis*, "sacred remembering." Catechesis needs to expose as false the dominant narratives that uphold these six characteristics of Western culture. The "communitarian-narrativist" approach advocated by Alasdair MacIntyre, Stanley Hauerwas, John Westerhoff, and Walter Brueggemann is an example of anamnesis.

Counternarrative alone, however, is not adequate. The problem is that our daily lives become *patterned* after technology, consumerism, militarism, moralism, therapeutism, and deism, a pattern that is incommensurate with the pattern of the Incarnation and the pattern of the cross. This complex of seductive societal stories—as well as the rituals, learned behaviors, and acts of allegiance—have been embraced by the church itself too frequently.

Therefore, practices of *ascesis*, "sacred resistance" and "sacred dehabituation," must be added to practices of *anamnesis*.[17] Given that formation into Western culture takes many, many years, it would be naïve to think that deformation from the patterns and practices of Western culture and reformation into the patterns and practices of Christian faith could happen in a matter of weeks or even months. Kreider's call to extensive catechesis somberly recognizes the power of non-Christian formation, yet it also speaks to the "patient vigor"[18] of *anamnesis* and *ascesis* together, which can lead to formation into the pattern of Jesus life and the kingdom of reconciliation.

It would be easy to interpret Christian counter-formation as being anticultural. Christian formation is countercultural by definition, in the sense that it is about being "other-centered." But to simply be against culture still allows culture to set the agenda and is not consistent with God's reconciling work in the world. Rather, Christians are called to identify, articulate, and pattern their lives

---

[17] Brian Mahan, Michael Warren and David White, *Awakening Youth Discipleship: Christian Resistance in a Consumer Culture* (Eugene, OR: Cascade Books, 2008).

[18] Albert Borgmann, *Crossing the Postmodern Divide* (Chicago: University of Chicago Press, 1992).

after the new center, the lordship of Jesus and God's kingdom of reconciliation.

: Shana Peachey Boshart

I had the privilege of hearing Alan Kreider twice present his research on catechesis in the early church, in November of 2006 when he spoke at our church, and again at a pastor/spouse retreat in April 2007. That same spring, I was fortunate to be a student in Alan's seminary class, "Mission and Peace." As conference youth minister for Central Plains Mennonite Conference, I was interested in how Alan's research and insights on catechesis might apply to our context.

Alan presented a long list of objectives and tasks that ought to be included in catechesis. The list suggested two main goals for catechesis: (1) differentiating between the two paradigms—secular and Christian—that are operant in the catechumen's life, and (2) giving catechumens the tools by which to live according to the Christian paradigm.

While the early church offered catechesis to pagan adults, my concern was for youth raised in the church. What is the difference, I wondered, between Christian formation and catechesis? I concluded that the goals for catechesis suggested by Alan's list are the same goals we have for the Christian formation of the church's children. Catechesis "trains people to think and live as Christians and looks forward to baptism as a time of joyful arrival." Yes, and our question in the church regarding children is, when does it begin? I submit that it begins at birth, and that what we do at home, in worship, in Sunday school, Bible school, and other church settings counts as catechesis.

What is needed is a more acute awareness that part of Christian formation is to help children both to understand the difference between kingdom and culture and to choose the kingdom over culture. In our Midwestern Mennonite context, we are hardly aware of the extent to which we have become acculturated. I often think of the proverbial frog in the pot of water, swimming comfortably in the water as it heats up, blissfully unaware that the water will soon be too hot to escape.

Alan's insights on catechesis have given me clarity on the goals of Christian formation, but if the goals of catechesis are the same as the goals of Christian formation, when does one take aside candidates for baptismal preparation, and what does one do with them that is different from what has been done already?

Experience suggests that the need to call people out and prepare them for church membership is just as urgent now as it was in the early church. Even faithful churchgoers need to be reminded that American culture and the kingdom of God are radically at odds. We need to be reminded that living in the way of Jesus requires constant, conscious choices, and that these choices will make us odd in the eyes of the world.

Alan's research makes clear the enormous challenge of catechizing our members, and it makes me rethink the goals and methods of Christian formation in children, youth, and adults.

9

Friendship
Find fellow travelers

Though we haven't written a lot about friendship, these paragraphs give voice to assumptions that have permeated our lives in the past thirty years. Sometimes people neglect to articulate things central to their life, so we will attempt to do that in speaking about friendship and hospitality.

Friendship is never easy. As David Wood has observed, this is especially true in our era. The pressurized, individualized, and sexualized world we live in is a hostile environment for the growth of friendship. Contemporary theologians exacerbate the problem, diminishing friendship because they assume that agape *must be more central than* philia *to the lives of Christians.*[1]

But we note in the Bible that Jesus calls his disciples friends (John 15:14–15). And although Paul was rarely called a friend (but see Acts 19:31), his letters end with salutations to and recommendations of people for whom he has the commitment of friendship—a sense of affectionate concern, enjoyment, respect, and solidarity that makes people present to our minds and hearts even when they are separated from us by time and space. Friendship of this sort grows with time. It involves a shared history, often with ups and downs. It involves fidelity—a persistence to remain in relationship even when distance might cause us to allow ties to grow slack.

To us, friendship—with Jesus and with other people—is what life is about. It is receiving another person; being present to another person; receiving the other's life, wisdom, hope, and pain. In friendship we are enabled to pass on to the other the welcome that we have received from

---

[1] David J. Wood, "The Recovery and the Promise of Friendship," *Princeton Seminary Bulletin*, n.s., 28, no. 2 (2007): 165–80.

Christ. "Welcome one another, just as Christ has welcomed you, for the glory of God" (Rom. 15:7). Sometimes we have met people with whom this friendship has not developed. The contact may have been intense, but it was fleeting. We or they may have moved on before the relationship could mature, or dissonances of views and lifestyles may have made relating difficult.

But with many people we have experienced friendship. In friendship there is an affinity that is reciprocal, that is the product of shared delights and longings, and that has joy as its mysterious by-product. Friendship of this sort is something we cannot demand and hardly dare expect. But in our experience, friendship is a gift with which God repeatedly surprises us. For this we give thanks.

We have experienced friendship in many ways. We have found it in churches, which at their best have been societies of friends. We have found it with people with whom we have traveled—often by walking, at times by working for a common cause. There is something about a shared journey that builds friendship. We have found it with people who have offered us spiritual support and moral discernment—we think especially here of the accountability group that met with us regularly during our last five years in England.

And we have found friendship in a special way at table where people share food and life. In our early years in London, we learned that friendship grew as we did what the early Anabaptist "Congregational Order" prescribed: after the worship, "serve a soup." We learned that friendship grew as we worshiped and ate together, and as we washed up following the meal (not prescribed by the order!). We also experienced friendship growing at table later in our England years, in our Oxford house church, "Group." We were learning by disciplined practice that there is something eucharistic about friendship, that breaking bread together, with Christ as host, has bonded us to others in love and made the table a sacred, hospitable place.

Hospitality, we have discovered, is central. Yet we always knew it. It was what our parents modeled and taught us. Their kitchens and dining room tables were constantly surrounded by people from the neighborhood and from all parts of the world. Deep in the Mennonite tradition and evident from the start of the Anabaptist movement is the hosting of family, neighbors, refugees, and itinerants. This hospitality was how the movement originally functioned, and it is how it has survived—Menno Simons on his Low Countries circuit, Hutterian missionaries spreading out across central Europe, and innumerable acts of radical hospitality in our own time. Hospitality is a core Anabaptist practice, as central as it was to the New Testament church.

In this, giving hospitality is crucial, but so is receiving it. This two-way interplay is a recurring theme in the New Testament. "I will come to your house," Jesus said, shockingly, to the centurion (Matt. 8:7). Jesus sent his disciples to stay in the homes of others (Luke 10:5). Paul and his colleagues constantly showed up and imposed themselves on generous hosts. In this way we Christians reflect God's hospitality toward us (Rom. 15:7).

We have experienced both movements of this interplay—accommodating guests in our own home as well as being the guests of others, in which we listen to our hosts and eat their food. It isn't always clear who are the "angels unaware" (Heb. 13:2)—those offering hospitality or those receiving it. So hospitality builds friendship, and friendship is at the heart of the life that we share in Christ.[2]

....

: Brian Haymes and Sean Winter

The fact that Alan and Ellie Kreider have never explored the theme of friendship explicitly in their writing comes initially as a surprise. As they recognize, the likely explanation lies in the very centrality of friendship for their life together as a couple and then as shared with so many others. Here, as so often with the Kreiders, the letter has been "written on [their] hearts, to be known and read by all" (2 Cor. 3:2).

Yet it is also true that the written word of scripture bears witness to the importance of friendship. It may be helpful to take a moment to offer a fuller account of that testimony, for it takes us beyond those texts where Jesus calls his followers friends and leads

---

[2] Alan and Eleanor Kreider, written for this book, October 2009.

us to the heart of the missio Dei, God's covenantal love for a people and through them for a world.

Friendship in the Bible leads us to the heart of God's mission

The drama begins with Abraham, named as a friend of God in later tradition (Isa. 41:8; James 2:23). The call of Abraham, clearly understood in the Pentateuch to signify a new start for humanity following Genesis 1–11, is not just a summons into a new way of life or a new vocation. God grants to the "ancestor of many nations" a new identity, expressed in a new name and rooted in the new relationship between God and God's people established in the covenantal ceremony described in Genesis 17:1–8.

Covenantal friendship thus establishes a reciprocal but asymmetrical relationship between God and God's people—God promises to be God, and Abraham is called to trust that promise (Gen. 15:6). This relationship is later expressed neatly in the repeated "covenant formulary" of Israel's testimony: "I will be their God, and they shall be my people" (Jer. 31:33; see also Gen. 17:8; Exod. 6:7; Lev. 26:12). Later Moses, acting in a representative capacity (see Exod. 32:12–17) is allowed to meet with YHWH, who speaks to him "face to face, as one speaks to a friend" (Exod. 33:11).[3] The notion that friendship is a way of speaking about the divine-human encounter is also reflected in Jewish wisdom traditions. Wisdom herself "in every generation . . . passes into holy souls and makes them friends of God, and prophets" (Wisdom of Solomon 7:27).

It comes as no surprise that while the language of friendship is rare in the New Testament, not least with reference to our relationship with God, it does appear in those texts that owe a debt to the wisdom tradition. James 4:4 reminds us that friendship with the world constitutes enmity with God. More positively, in John's Gospel Jesus offers specific teaching to indicate that members of the disciple community are named as friends (John 15:12–17).

---

[3] See Jacqueline C. Lapsley, "Friends with God?: Moses and the Possibility of Covenantal Friendship," *Interpretation* 58, no. 2 (2004): 117–29.

As the context makes clear, Jesus' words here are first and foremost a description of the participation of the disciples in the relationship of love that exists between God as Father and Jesus the Son. Jesus, as the divine revealer of God's love for the world, expresses that love as he lays down his life for his friends. Pauline scholars also recognize that the fundamental structures of Paul's restatement of Jewish covenantal theology can be expressed, via the language of *koinōnia*, in terms that evoke the Greco-Roman notion of friendship in human social relations.[4]

Therefore we are faced with biblical traditions that use friendship as a way of speaking about divine love *ad extra* (to use the terms of classic theological discussion). We are friends with God because God's love is directed toward us and gathers us into relationship. This notion is subsequently taken up as an important though oft-neglected theme in the Christian tradition.[5] But the focus on divine-human friendship inevitably leads us to consider our friendship with each other. There is no more beautiful evocation of this deep connection than the opening of the book of Ruth, where Ruth commits herself to her mother-in-law in words that reflect the covenant promises:

> Where you go, I will go;
> Where you lodge, I will lodge;
> your people shall be my people,
> and your God, my God (Ruth 1:16).

Here, the commitment of one to be with another is understood to be a sharing in God's promise to be for humanity. The vertical and the horizontal dimensions of friendship belong together.

Thus, the point we wish to make is that divine love is constitutive of human love. The asymmetry of Israel's covenantal language

---

[4] For a survey, see John T. Fitzgerald, "Paul and Friendship," in *Paul in the Greco-Roman World: A Handbook*, ed. J. Paul Sampley (Harrisburg, PA: Trinity Press International, 2003), 319–43; and note the theological reading of Philippians in Stephen E. Fowl, *Philippians* (Grand Rapids, MI: Eerdmans, 2005).

[5] The best single volume survey of this neglected aspect of Christian tradition is E. D. H. Carmichael, *Friendship: Interpreting Christian Love* (London: T & T Clark International, 2004).

reflects the conviction that the divine-human encounter shapes the form of the community that is the result of it. To talk of friendship is to speak theologically as well as ethically.

Vertical and horizontal dimensions of friendship belong together

This developing biblical picture of friendship—a fundamentally relational reality with inseparable vertical and horizontal dimensions—may well cause us to reflect on the nature of God in Trinity. Not that we want to suggest a model of the Trinity as the associating of three close friends! However, Christian theology does speak of the life of God as one of constantly outflowing love between the Father, the Son, and the Spirit, one to another. What we witness here is not loving as a matter of obligation so much as the expression of inexhaustible intercommunion and mutual indwelling (*perichoresis*).

Friendships, marked by both *agape* and *philia*, might therefore be understood theologically to be a form of participation in the life and love of God. So Jürgen Moltmann, exploring what it means for disciples to live in the rule of God, asserts, "Ultimately a freedom is experienced in the Spirit which goes even beyond the relationship of being a son—friendship with God. They share in the grief and joy of God. The 'friends' of God no longer live 'under' God but *with* God and *in* God. They have become 'one' with God (John 17:21)."[6] Thus it is impossible to share the life of God without living in love toward our neighbors, those who with us inhabit the world God loves so much. So, loving our neighbors, especially our friends, might well be understood as participating in the divine love for all humankind.

This theological dynamic, between the vertical and horizontal dimensions of Christian faith and practice, is ubiquitous in the biblical witness. Romans 15:7 is a wonderful example of just this dynamic. It is also a feature of the Kreiders' writing, and as their paragraphs above make clear, of their living.

---

[6] Jürgen Moltmann, *History and the Triune God: Contributions to Trinitarian Theology*, trans. John Bowden (London: SCM Press 1991), 25.

This dynamic is a marked by relating, reciprocity, giving, and receiving. It is real in experience, and such friendships matter to us deeply. That we could not easily conceive of life without friends suggests that something vital for human health and salvation is here. Friendships therefore involve some basic human aspects, such as liking one another and being attracted to another.[7]

Friendship as mutuality and reciprocity calls for accountability to God and to others

But a theological understanding of friendship as mutual, outgoing, sustaining love suggests that grace and trust are fundamental features of these relationships. To have a friend is to receive a graceful gift. Trust is possible where those involved recognize a claim on them as a matter of integrity and identity.

Theologically, this is a feature of covenant—God keeps the promises at the heart of covenant, and God's people live in covenant insofar as they trust the word and ways of God. To break trust, to behave in unfriendly ways, is to be false to one's vocation and identity, both for God and for humankind. Thus within a Christian understanding, this crucial claim, which is the ground of trust, is the claim of God to whom all are accountable. The theme of *Gelassenheit*, so basic to an Anabaptist understanding of discipleship, affirms the necessity of mutual disciplining as our friends hold us accountable to our one calling in Christ.[8]

The ecclesial and ethical implications of this theology are far reaching. For example, spiritual growth often involves the ministry of a soul friend, a spiritual director. The idea that we should make thoroughly individual retreats seriously misleads us when it comes to growth in the knowledge of God. For that we need one another. Friendships are a form of social community, challenging some prevalent solitary models of spirituality and integrity. Therefore the calling of the church might well be understood in terms

---

[7] See the discussion by Paul J. Wadell in chapter 2 of *Becoming Friends: Worship, Justice, and the Practice of Christian Friendship* (Grand Rapids, MI: Brazos Press, 2002).

[8] See the discussion by C. Arnold Snyder, *Following in the Footsteps of Christ: The Anabaptist Tradition* (London: Darton, Longman and Todd, 2004).

of fostering friendships. If that is so, we need to give attention to the ways we worship, to creating space and time for people to be together, to the shape and use of our buildings—all of which can enable friendships to grow.

To be healthy, friendships need to have space, but for them to flourish, they must avoid any temptation to exclusivity.[9] This is true for marriage: it is nothing if the partners are not best friends, but it will flounder eventually if the partners are each other's only friends. Being open to the other, especially the stranger, is not a threat to friendship in Christ but rather is one form of this friendship's genuine expression.

And Alan and Ellie are quite right to highlight the theological, ecclesial, missional, and personal importance of hospitality as an embodied practice that creates and nurtures true friendship. Their emphasis on shared meals can hardly be overestimated, so deeply embedded is it in the Bible story. No wonder the Kreiders suggest that something sacramental is going on here. At table, with others, grace is given and shared. The things of the earth, including our own bodies, are taken up into the action of God. A number of groups in the United Kingdom meet regularly around a meal table, to share a meal; to listen to scripture; and to mutually support, guide, admonish, and encourage one another in discipleship: these practices remain an important result of the Kreiders' ministry among us.

For the sake of God's mission, the church needs a politics of friendship

Finally, it can be argued that it is for the sake of its mission—or rather, its participation in the mission of God—that the church needs to develop what Jacques Derrida calls a "politics of friendship."[10] Many in our world today are looking for forms of community and patterns

---

[9] This point is carefully made and explored by Miroslav Volf in *Exclusion and Embrace: A Theological Exploration of Identity, Otherness and Reconciliation* (Nashville, TN: Abingdon Press, 1996).

[10] Jacques Derrida, *Politics of Friendship*, trans. George Collins (London: Verso, 1997).

of relationship that go beyond the conventional and sometimes problematic aspects of "family" life. The full inclusion of women, as well as lesbian, gay, bisexual, and transgendered people, is often obstructed by some of the patriarchal and androcentric assumptions that pervade church life, assumptions that are often implicitly and sometimes explicitly reinforced by talk of the church as a family.[11]

Many younger people now understand their friendships to be their most significant relationships, a recognition sometimes prompted by deeply traumatic experiences of family life. The way the church community welcomes the elderly and the disabled might also be assisted by some theological reflection on the nature of friendship.[12] Fears that such reflection could reinforce the sense of the church as an exclusive community of the like-minded are overcome when we realize that the divine friendship in which we participate as a society of friends is always reaching out in welcome and embrace of the stranger.[13]

Bonhoeffer's poetic meditation on the importance of friendship comes to mind at the conclusion of these reflections:

Far or near
in success or failure
the one recognizes in the other
the true helper

---

[11] For a discussion of some of these issues, see Elisabeth Moltmann-Wendel, *Rediscovering Friendship*, trans. John Bowden (London: SCM Press, 2000); Marilyn Friedman, *What Are Friends For? Feminist Perspectives on Personal Relationships and Moral Theory* (Ithaca, NY: Cornell University Press, 1993); and Mark Vernon, *The Philosophy of Friendship* (London: Palgrave Macmillan, 2006).

[12] See Stanley Hauerwas and Laura Yordy, "Captured in Time: Friendship and Aging," in *A Better Hope: Resources for a Church Confronting Capitalism, Democracy, and Postmodernity*, by Stanley Hauerwas (Grand Rapids, MI: Brazos Press, 2000), 117–29; and the essays in *Critical Reflections on Stanley Hauerwas' Theology of Disability: Disabling Society, Enabling Theology*, ed. John Swinton (Binghampton, NY: Haworth Pastoral, 2004).

[13] The works by Friedman and Derrida, noted above, both serve to deconstruct the idea of friendship as an exclusive relationship.

> toward freedom
> and humanity.[14]

Not only does Bonhoeffer write this poem in such a way as to connect human and divine friendship, but the prison location of its composition reminds us that friendship is deeply entangled with the cost of discipleship. Indeed, friendship, we suggest, is the form that discipleship takes in community as we live together in response to divine welcome and in obedience to the one who calls us friends. Alan and Ellie Kreider have embodied the "true helper toward freedom and humanity" for each other, for the two of us, and for all those who count them as friends.

⋮ Michele Hershberger

Some days I felt like I was in a tough spot when it concerned friendship. I was on a one-year teaching assignment at LCC International University in Klaipeda, Lithuania. How does one make friends in nine months? I taught students in an eastern European context where people don't usually talk about their faith and regard with suspicion anything that looks like an ideology. The Bible classes I taught were required and sometimes seen as a barrier to the business degree to which students aspired. What did it mean to be a friend in this place? Was there such a thing as "missional friendship"?

In much the same way that Brian Haymes and Sean Winter have emphasized covenant, and Alan and Eleanor Krieder have lived out their friendships, I decided to risk doing friendship differently. This risk called for a continual supply of God's hospitality and friendship, in order to be friends with others, particularly in a setting dominated by new names and strange faces, and in light of the hostile remarks I heard at the beginning of the year about how

---

[14] Dietrich Bonhoeffer, "The Friend." The text, a translation (slightly altered here) and an excellent discussion can be found in Stanley Hauerwas, "'The Friend': Reflections on Friendship and Freedom," in *Who Am I?: Bonhoeffer's Theology through His Poetry*, ed. Bernd Wannenwetsch (London: T & T Clark, 2009), 91–113.

worthless this class would be. I needed a foundation of being God's beloved in order to have the wherewithal not to react to these challenges. And as is the case with covenant, each participant needed the freedom to choose this friendship.

As I looked at my students, I decided to give that gift. I committed myself to respect them and care about them, no matter what they thought about Jesus and the Bible. I tried to teach within the paradox of authority and gentleness. And I learned that friendship has value at all levels. Some of my new friends wanted—and needed—me to be a person who just talked about the weather. Others wanted a more intimate relationship. My needs were similar.

The messiest part of this missional friendship was my relationships with my students. How do I teach differently because of Jesus? How can I be an appropriate friend and also an appropriate instructor? I knew I had to step into that messiness. I asked students about their weekends—and was really interested in their responses. I was the first one to arrive for class and the last to leave. We shared stories about culture shock. I didn't bluff—if I didn't know an answer, I admitted it. I laughed at myself when I made a mistake. Without overstepping my boundaries, I asked for their help when I had a bad day. I took a risk—a risk that they might misunderstand me or try to manipulate me. But the alternative was worse—controlling the relationship so much that we couldn't be present to each other the way Jesus was present with his friends.

And it happened—missional friendship. It was not missional in that I had a secret agenda to convert my students. That's manipulation, not friendship. On the other hand, I wanted my students to feel safe enough to talk to me about faith—on their terms. It was missional in that my own needs were sufficiently met—through my own friendship with God—so I could truly be there for them. It meant being appropriately vulnerable, because God was helping me be authentic. Ironically—or perhaps understandably—on the days I was more connected to God's hospitality, I was also more able to be there for the other, able to respond in ways that met their needs and not just mine.

: Catherine Horton

In 1989 I moved, with my husband and our three young children, to live in Kirkby-in-Ashfield, Nottinghamshire, a small town that had once been a thriving center of the coal mining industry. The town's livelihood was now sapped as a result of pit closures, the last one happening while we were there in the 1990s.

With four or five other families, we were involved in planting a church based around a council estate in the town. We met in one another's homes and in the local school and got to know folk in the neighborhood by knocking on doors and offering to pray for their needs. Friendship and nonreligious expression of our shared life in Christ were the key values.

A young family lived next door to us. When one family was away on holiday, the other would keep an eye on their home. One night when we were away, they spotted our back door wide open, came over to check the house, and must have disturbed burglars—who fled with some belongings, leaving the contents of many drawers and cupboards scattered on the floor.

Our neighbor knew some of our friends in the church, so in addition to ringing the police, she also rang our friends the next day to tell them what had happened. After the police had done the necessary checks, these church members came around with others and completely tidied up the house for us, bringing flowers to welcome us home—which resulted in our returning to a far cleaner and tidier home than the one we had left! The church friends decided not to spoil our camping holiday in France by calling to tell us what had happened. But to ensure that the house remained safe, a few of the men in the church had slept on our living room floor until our return. We were, of course, totally unaware of these angels!

Soon after our return home, our neighbor ran out of her house to greet us, the expression on her face telling us that something special had happened. With tears in her eyes she told us the whole story, finishing with "Nobody loves me like that, except my mum . . . I want to join your church!"

Over the next few days, we spent time together as she explained how she could not believe the kindness of our friends in the church. She had seen love in action in a most practical and committed way, and had been bowled over. There was no doubt that by getting to know our friends better and sharing in their kindness, this neighbor had participated in the life and love of God. In her own words, "I could not believe all they did for you—and you've only been here five years." It was a natural step for her to understand and receive God's love into her life, and she committed her life to God. A few months later her husband did the same. As this story illustrates, the calling of the church might well be understood in terms of fostering friendships.

10

Peace church
Transform the Christian community

Peace, Peter told Cornelius, was what Jesus evangelized (Acts 10:36). Ephesians 2:14 says of Jesus, "He himself is our peace." Jesus is the peacemaker. To know what peace means, we don't argue politics or theology; we look at Jesus. We tell the story of Jesus. We listen to Jesus. We watch Jesus in action—Jesus with his friends, Jesus in conflict, Jesus loving his enemies, Jesus on the cross, Jesus making peace. The church's task, from generation to generation, is to ponder the story and teachings of Jesus and to pass on Jesus' ways.

Paul saw his task in this light—to invite people to "follow my example as I follow the example of Christ" (1 Cor. 11:1). Jesus' ways, lived by his followers, would become ways to be lived—and copied—by others. As Paul said to the Christians in Philippi, "Whatever you have learned or received or heard from me, or seen in me—put it into practice. And the God of peace will be with you" (Phil. 4:9). Jesus, the embodiment of the peace of God, is alive. Paul says, "He himself is our peace," and he shows us what peace is all about.

Peace is central to biblical faith. It is impossible to exaggerate this ... In the Bible peace is not an extra-cost option. It is central. The only reason that we Gentiles (Indonesian Gentiles or Argentinean Gentiles or Canadian Gentiles) are in the church is God's miraculous act of peacemaking in Christ. So peace is for the whole church. In fact, peace is a word that we could use to designate our churches. When people ask us, "Tell me about your church," we could say, "We're a culture of peace. God is a God of peace, and we're learning what peace means. It's exciting. Would you like to come and see?" ...

It's not completely clear what it will mean for a church to become a culture of peace. It will not be easy, and the changes required will be numerous. They will take time—because essentially we are looking at a process of cultural change within the church. And such a change of culture can only take place over the medium- to long-term, through a range of strategies sustained over time . . . Some of these necessary changes are: new attitudes and reflexes that enable a constructive handling of differences, speaking truth in love, good listening, expecting God to bring insight through the other's experience, holding each other accountable, and believing that the Holy Spirit is at work to bring about Jesus' way of peace on the earth—now.

All of this requires that a church that is becoming a culture of peace must undertake two fundamental tasks: empowering the individuals in the church and empowering the structures of the church.

First of all, empowering individuals. How do we shape the character of individual Christians to become peacemakers? Through the educational and worship practices of the church. For example, we need to evaluate the materials we use in teaching baptismal candidates, in classes for new church members, or in children and adult Sunday schools. Do these teaching materials equip our people, both adults and children, to live the peaceful way of life? Do they impart the necessary knowledge and skills for peacemaking?

Peace education in the church and in Christian schools is also vital. We must train our pastors, our elders, deacons, and all church members with the knowledge and skills for nonviolent conflict transformation. We need to design curricula for peace education and to study biblical peace texts closely and expectantly in all areas of our church life—including in our worship. Have we made peace a central theme in our worship? Do we regularly preach the gospel of peace? Do we pray earnestly for peace? Does our church calendar include a Peace Month or a Peace Sunday?

Second, empowering the church's structures. Have we established a procedure in the church to address and transform in nonviolent ways the conflict that emerges inside and outside the church? Churches that do not have such procedures risk trying to hide the conflict or burying it. Hidden conflicts can grow and become like time bombs that can destroy the whole church at a later time.

Many churches have committees, each one dealing with particular concerns or interests: youth, women, mission, worship. Perhaps the church should have a peace committee. It would be in charge of educating and training church members for peacemaking both inside and outside the church. It could serve both the church and the wider society through advocacy and mediation to transform conflict whenever needed.

There is no master plan for the transformation of our churches so that they can become cultures of peace. Each church will learn things in its own order, in its own time. But any church that sets out to transform itself to become a culture of peace will be on a journey. Gerard Hughes, a Scottish spiritual writer who has gone on many pilgrimages, has stated this wisely: "It is better to travel than to arrive." [1] *Woe to the church that arrives! It will not be a culture of peace. But in greeting the Messiah, Zechariah was surely right. God's mercy was at work "to shine on those living in darkness and in the shadow of death, [and] to guide our feet into the path of peace" (Luke 1:79). And this way will transform not only reflexes of Christians and the "domestic" life of their churches; it will also transform their churches' witness and life in the world.* [2]

....

⁝ Noel Moules

Peace church is a phrase so simple, who can misunderstand it? It is tantalizingly attractive, and at the same time quietly disturbing. It has the touch of genius about it.

Peace church as a phrase has been in use for some time. People speak of "historic peace churches" when referring to the Anabaptist, Brethren, and Quaker traditions of refusing to use violence or to

---

[1] Gerard Hughes, *In Search of a Way: Two Journeys of Discovery* (Rome and Sydney: E. J. Dwyer, 1978), 75.

[2] Reprinted from Alan Kreider, Eleanor Kreider, and Paulus Widjaja, *A Culture of Peace: God's Vision for the Church.* © by Good Books (www.GoodBooks.com). Used by permission. All rights reserved.

take part in war.[3] Subtly and psychologically this usage has marginalized the phrase, implying that it has little to do with mainstream churches with their clearly established "just war" theologies and traditions. Alan and Eleanor Kreider have been right to give the expression *peace church* a much greater and broader focus.

It is time to embrace the full meaning of biblical shalom

Peace is the gospel. This is a statement we need to devote time to pondering, letting its full implications take hold of us. We have heard Peter describing it to Cornelius as "the message God sent to the people of Israel, telling the good news of peace through Jesus Christ" (Acts 10:36; NIV-UK). In whatever way the evangel may be described—the kingdom of God, forgiveness of sins, and much else—this single word *peace* distills and communicates not simply its essence but its totality. The gospel is "the gospel of peace" (Eph. 6:15).

Nevertheless, the word *peace* can mean different things to different people—anything from personal tranquility to the absence of war. So what does it mean when it is both modeled and proclaimed by Jesus? The word Jesus would have used in Hebrew is *shalom*. His distinct use of this popular greeting, and the way it was understood in the early Christian community, become both the key to everyday living and the code unlocking the meaning of the universe. It is in fact the ultimate goal to which the whole cosmos in God is heading! It is everyday and practical and at the same time awesomely eschatological.

Shalom is best translated by the word *wholeness*. It is first and foremost about relationship: touching, embracing, and energizing every possible life link. We are to live in shalom with God, with every other human being, with the whole of the natural world, living and inert, and with and within ourselves.

Furthermore, tracing the use of shalom through the scriptures reveals three primary recurring characteristics. These come to

---

[3] "Historic Peace Churches" began to be popularly used following the Conference of Pacifist Churches first held in Bluffton, Ohio, in August 1922. See www.gameo.org/encyclopedia/encyclopedia/contents/conference_of_pacifist_churches.

serve as a measuring stick or plumb line by which we can determine the extent to which shalom is a present reality in any given situation: Shalom demands physical and material well-being and dignity for all. Shalom insists that every relationship is just and right. Shalom requires that each person has integrity and holiness in character.[4]

Church is the *ekklesia* community that responds to the call to live from a Jesus perspective. Peace church identifies this community as one that is motivated by and working toward all the qualities we have identified above, both within itself and in its mission to reach into wider society and creation. This being so, peace as shalom must not be viewed as merely a vital segment in some greater whole within the life of the local church; properly understood, peace *is* the whole—the foundation, the fabric, its totality.

Peace church is about a living and life-giving Jesus-centered culture

The Kreiders make this point powerfully in their use of the phase "a culture of peace." Peace church is much more than pursuing an idea, like a child chasing a butterfly on a summer's day. It is certainly much more than working to get church structures peace-shaped, where the emphasis is often on preserving rather than serving, on the static rather than the dynamic. Instead, peace church is about a living and life-giving Jesus-centered culture.

Culture is like the air we breathe; it gives our personal lives vitality, color, and texture, and it gives our communities variety, contours, and shape. It is impossible to live without, because the very act of living creates culture. It is an intricate web of being[5] that is both tactile and conceptual. Culture also shapes our inner

---

[4] These three primary characteristics of shalom, and the way I have presented them, are broadly based on ideas found in Perry Yoder, *Shalom: The Bible's Word for Salvation, Justice, and Peace* (Newton, KS: Faith and Life Press, 1987), 10–23; and Claus Westermann, "Peace (*Shalom*) in the Old Testament," in *The Meaning of Peace*, 2nd edition, ed. Perry Yoder and Willard Swartley (Elkhart, IN: Institute of Mennonite Studies, 2001), 37–70.

[5] The idea of culture being like a web is widely used, including by the Kreiders in Alan Kreider, Eleanor Kreider, and Paulus Widjaja, *A Culture of Peace: God's Vision for the Church*, 6.

structure and identity, touching our mind, emotions, and spirit. It influences the way we view the world and how we choose to engage with it.

A peace church focus on culture is important, because culture is something we actually work to create, and in return it creates us. It has been insightfully observed that "human beings are both the inventors and the inventions of culture."[6] This means that every local church, whatever its history or tradition, has the potential to become a peace church. Every culture is shaped by values. When that core value is shalom, its essential qualities will percolate through each fiber or membrane of the community, and from there into the surrounding environment. Jesus makes exactly this point when he speaks of yeast mixed into flour until it worked all through the dough (Luke 13:21).

How then do we cultivate[7] peace communities of faith?
Through transformed minds beginning from within. Peace church is, first and foremost, a way of thinking. It begins with our understanding, with *metanoia*, that Greek word referring to a change of mind that leads to a new way of living. It is about learning to perceive things with a Jesus focus and from a shalom perspective, and in the process fundamentally changing the way we view the world. What will flow from this shift will be a transformation of the very ethos[8] of our mindset and our experience of community. It is vital that the first step toward peace church begins from within, shaping minds that understand and hearts that are excited to embrace the vision.

Through voices within the community. How does it happen? It will of course come through the voices within the community—the teaching, preaching, prayer, worship, liturgy, and every other activity we do together, each of them yeasted with peace.

---

[6] David Augsburger, *Pastoral Counseling across Cultures* (Philadelphia: Westminster Press, 1986), 58.

[7] Note that the word *culture* comes from the Latin *cultura*, "cultivation."

[8] The Greek word *ethos* is another culture word with the sense of "custom and character" and closely linked to *ethikos* (ethics), referring to "behavior and character."

But beyond that, it is most important to listen for it in the coffee cup conversations—those spontaneous encounters where ideas and questions are shared between people about their personal experiences of experimenting with peace.

Through storytelling. Story is a vital key to peace transfiguration. Across the world's cultures, storytelling weaves together meaning, understanding, values, wisdom, and ethos within communities. Stories connect people to their roots in the past; they give them continuity with the present and in so doing strengthen their sense of security and identity, while at the same time exciting the hearer with hope about the future.

It is our ability as human beings to tell a story that most clearly distinguishes us from our creation companions in the animal world. Stories have the remarkable ability to capture the imagination of child and adult alike. Therefore, in shaping and nurturing a peace church, storytelling must be key. Storytelling has always been an important part of the Kreiders' focus.[9]

We have the big creation-salvation story, its sweeping arc bending through time, space, and eternity in a trajectory toward peace. This is the backdrop against which we tell biblical stories that model and teach authentic peace.[10] Added to this are the myriad global peace stories, mostly untold, that can inspire and instruct. Finally, but vitally, we must include those coffee cup conversations, honoring the animated accounts of people exploring and testing peace in the local neighborhood, actively interlacing them into the fabric of this shared story journey.

Through sharing together the food-laden table—the "peacemeal." Jesus leaves us one physical thing with which to build church: a table upon which there is food. Central to being a peace church is the meal we share in company with the risen Jesus:

---

[9] For just one example see Alan Kreider, Eleanor Kreider, and Paulus Widjaja, *A Culture of Peace*, 104–8.

[10] I am deeply mindful that for many people the biblical stories appear to speak more about violence than about peace. Peace church communities must grapple with this reality head-on, engaging with people's understanding and emotional struggle. We must demonstrate that shalom is the primary focus of truth and reality, but we must not ignore the violence passages, hoping they will disappear.

the peacemeal.[11] This food-laden table, with bread and wine as its focal point, is to be the centerpeace of the Christian community of faith. It is centripetal, drawing to it whoever is hungry, physically and spiritually, and is willing to come. An important word Jesus connects with this meal is "Remember": *We remember Jesus:* Jesus himself is our peace (Eph. 2:14), the one through whom God brings about the reconciliation of all things "by making peace through his blood, shed on the cross" (Col. 1:20; NIV-UK). Our focus is on him. *We re-member the community:* We look around at one another as the body of Christ. Hurts and broken relationships find healing and forgiveness, and those who are struggling find support as we reach out to one another in love. *We remember others:* Sharing this meal sensitizes us to the desperate need among humanity and within creation for the experience of shalom.

Through mission and service to the world. This being so, we discover that the peacemeal is also centrifugal; it sends us out into the world to proclaim the gospel of peace in word and deed. The blessing and instruction—Go in peace to love and serve the Lord!—that has concluded so many such meals down through the ages could not be clearer.

Peace church is about mission.[12] Jesus' command to us is unequivocal: "Go into all the world and preach the good news to all creation" (Mark 16:15; NIV-UK). We are also told, "Make every effort to live in peace with everyone and to be holy; without holiness no-one will see the Lord" (Heb. 12:14; NIV-UK). The first requirement in proclaiming peace is that the messenger-activist display that unique spiritual integrity that reflects the character of God. This integrity is what it means to be people of peace (Luke 10:6). Pursuing peace and holiness comes both from nurturing spiritual-

---

[11] This topic has been a major theme in the Kreiders' teaching and writing; see, for example, *A Culture of Peace*, 114–18; and more extensively, Eleanor Kreider, *Communion Shapes Character* (Scottdale, PA: Herald Press, 1997).

[12] One of the many strengths of the Kreiders' teaching on peace church has been their emphasis on mission and Christian engagement with the challenges that society presents. More than a third of their book *A Culture of Peace* directly addresses this theme.

ity within the community of faith itself and from actively working to establish shalom within the wider world.

As children of God we are called to be peacemakers (Matt. 5:9). This call implies two things—enormous physical and emotional energy as we wrestle to establish peace in seemingly intractable situations, paralleled by a commitment to love and gentleness, the hallmark of which is a total absence of violence.[13]

The gospel of shalom is salvation in the most complete sense

Central to the biblical vision of shalom is *mishpat*, the process of putting everything right. This concept contains both justice and judgment, a main focus of the peace church understanding of mission. It is to engage at every level with personal, social, and ecological challenges, "struggling with all [Christ's] energy, which so powerfully works in me" (Col. 1:29; NIV-UK). I frequently describe peace people as angels of judgment, working for the physical and material well-being and dignity of all, including the natural world, feeding, nurturing, enabling, and empowering. They struggle against injustice, seeking to mend and restore broken relationships. They seek ways to bring freedom and integrity to the inner depths of individuals in the power of the Spirit. Shalom is the gospel, because it is salvation in this most complete sense.

The totality of the gospel is peace for the whole of creation. Peace presented from a Jesus perspective is transcultural; planted among the people groups of the earth, it will always challenge and transform. We speak of a culture of peace, but that culture is by its very nature multicultural. Peace will enhance and affirm all that is beautiful and authentic in every culture and will transfigure what is not. This transformation should be true of the microcosm of each local peace church now, as of the macrocosm of "all things" ultimately.

In the words of John the Seer in Revelation, "After this I looked and there before me was a great multitude that no-one could count, from every nation, tribe, people and language . . . holding palm

---

[13] See Matt. 5:39, 44; 7:12.

branches in their hands. And they cried out in a loud voice, 'Salvation belongs to our God' . . . Then I heard every creature in heaven and on earth and under the earth and on the sea, and all that is in them, singing" (Rev. 7:9–10; 5:13; NIV-UK). This is the final and universal culmination of what peace church is truly all about.

⠸ Paulus Widjaja

When Alan and Eleanor Kreider talk about church identity, they are not talking about rites or rules but about the roots of the church. They have profoundly pointed out that there is no other way to explain our identity as Christians than by referring to Jesus Christ, our root. And when we refer to Jesus Christ, there is no other possibility than affirming that Jesus is peace (2 Thess. 3:16). As Christians, we may differ from one another in how we worship God or structure our church governance. The real issue any Christian should struggle with, however, is not about which worship or church governance is truest, but about how our worship or church governance can reflect our faith rooted in Jesus Christ, who is peace. Who we are takes precedence over what we do. This is what the Kreiders have reminded us. Peace is the faith quality that should give shape to Christian identity, regardless of the different rites and rules that churches practice.

Here is an example from the Sermon on the Mount (Matt. 5–7), the most preached text in early Christianity, which elaborates the logic. This text is preceded by the story of Jesus' inauguration as the Son of God (Matt. 3:17) and Jesus' temptation, in which the devil asks, "*If* you are the Son of God . . ." (Matt. 4:3, 6). The devil questions Jesus' identity. Jesus has to prove it. But how? According to the devil, Jesus must prove his identity by demonstrating his power. This is the only way the world knows. Jesus, however, does not follow this usual rule of the game. Instead he gives new qualifications for one to be called Son of God. He elaborates these in the Sermon on the Mount.

What Jesus says in the Sermon on the Mount is not a prescription for becoming children of God; it is about the *way* to become children of God. It is not primarily imperative but indicative. It is first of all about the root, the identity, not about rites and rules. The concept of "human being" is defined by the criteria of what *good* human being is. Goodness is tied to the truest essence of human being. What human being ought to be must be understood in light of what good human being is. This is not to say that the indicative automatically turns into the imperative, nor can the imperative be directly deducted from the indicative. But the indicative always shapes the imperative. "There is a kind of 'isness' to the 'oughtness' in that the ought is what in fact we are."[14]

"Blessed are the peacemakers, for they will be called children of God" (Matt. 5:9), for instance, shows (indicative) that a human being is one who makes peace, not one who makes others enemies, excludes others, brings harm to others, kills others, etc. The ultimate question Jesus wants to answer is not, what should we do? but, what kind of person should we become? This is the question of roots, not rites and rules.

⁞ Cyneatha Millsaps

I grew up in a multicultural community. I was blessed to have Blacks, whites, and Latinos in my neighborhood and school. The neighborhood I grew up in was similar to many throughout America in the mid-1960s. The neighborhood was white until Blacks and others migrated in. When the migration happened, whites moved out and started other neighborhoods. What made my neighborhood unique was the fact that in the early 1970s a group of whites moved *into* the neighborhood instead of out. Their decision to engage a multicultural community was profound and life-changing for them and for the inhabitants of the neighborhood. It was their gift of engagement that produces a glimpse into the peace church.

The group that infiltrated my neighborhood created an intentional community following Jesus' call to rise to a higher standard

---

[14] Stanley Hauerwas, *Character and the Christian Life: A Study in Theological Ethics* (Notre Dame: University of Notre Dame Press, 1994), 209.

of living: nonviolence, social justice, and love of neighbor as self. Though this white Christian group managed to create unity in a minority neighborhood, I am often frustrated with members of the Christian church, because all too often their walk diverges from their talk. If we are truly followers of Christ, why is there so much violence, abuse, loneliness, hunger, and despair in our world? We are called to be peacemakers and comforters, to manifest the love of God.

Noel Moules describes peace as shalom, justice, and care for all concerned. In order for peace to become a reality, we must invite the idea of sacrifice. Jesus, who gave the ultimate sacrifice of his life, stated that "greater love has no one than this: to lay down one's life for one's friends" (John 15:13). In order for the peace church actually to be the peace church, the body of Christ must sacrifice: Leave our comfortable neighborhoods, schools, jobs—and yes, the four walls of our churches—and move to those places and people we consider less desirable. Abandon our power and privilege and engage the other on their turf. Take that spirit of peace and love with us. Stand in a nonviolent manner when violence may be all around us. "Even though I walk through the valley of the shadow of death, I will fear no evil, for you are with me" (Ps. 23:4; NIV-UK).

Simply, the point is to act on the faith that was presented as an example through Jesus Christ, as did the intentional community that moved into my neighborhood when I was a child. They were following the call of God to be a light to the world. They took what they had and shared it with one another and with their new community. The impact was such that it transformed the community to one of peace, respect, understanding, and love for one another.

What the Kreiders and Noel Moules are explaining is the notion that the peace church requires action, sacrifice, and trust in God. We have to be willing to give something up. In following Christ's example we have to walk by faith to bring peace to a church, to a neighborhood, and ultimately to the world.

11

The early churches
Walk in the ancient paths

Whatever the benefits of Christendom—and there were many—we today are no longer living in Christendom. The grand edifice built on inducement and compulsion has crumbled, and most people in the West have stopped going to church. Some people in fact now view themselves explicitly as pagan. These people view Christianity as a kind of parenthesis in Western history, which will inevitably be replaced by a religion that is more authentically European— paganism. Those of us who believe otherwise are aware that Christianity is on trial in the West. If the church survives, it will not be because of flattery or battery, "not by might, nor by power" (Zech. 4:6), but because of God's Spirit who is enabling Christians to emerge not as mere residents but, as in the early centuries, as resident aliens, purveyors of good news to our time.

This is a daunting challenge. With an unprecedented thoroughness our culture catechizes us in beliefs hostile to Christianity . . . We are enmeshed in a culture of violence, of endless dissatisfaction, of the promise of instant gratification, of limitless sexual expression. In the supermarket, as well as in Soho, we are assailed by addictions and compulsions. And in this setting we Christians are called to advocate the gospel of Jesus Christ and to invite people to true life in him.

In view of the paganism of our times, we would seem to have much in common with the pre-Christendom Christians. I believe that we do. But our circumstances are also very different. We are separated from them not only by seventeen hundred years but also by Christendom. In my experience most people today view Christians not as advocates of something new and exciting but rather as blinkered defenders of views that are old, which have been tried, and which have failed. They may differ about whether our Christian churches and institutions are benign or malign, but they do largely agree that they are backward-looking and irrelevant. For us, I believe, Christendom is a missiological problem.

In this setting, the early Christians cannot tell us what to do. They didn't have everything worked out, and on many points we, for good reason, would not want to copy them. The early Christians can, however, ask us some questions. "At work or at home," they might well ask us, "are you known to your neighbors? Are you known as members of a superstitio, *a deviation from the norms of accepted behavior? Are you distinctive because of Jesus, whose teachings and way offer you perspectives and ways of living that are new?*

"And how about your congregations? In the way that they function and worship, are they becoming communities of peace and freedom which are evidences of the truth of the gospel? And your catechesis: as you prepare people for baptism, are you equipping them to live freely in the face of the addictions and compulsions of your time? Are you teaching them new narratives and new folkways, so that they are being re-formed into people who are distinctively Christian? Finally, in your worship, what do your rites (for you all have them) say about your churches' beliefs and priorities? Are your rites strong and living, enabling you to address the issues that really trouble your communities? Do you evaluate your worship primarily by how it makes you feel, or by the extent to which it shapes your character—as communities of faith and as individual Christians—so you look like Jesus Christ?"

In German the early church is called die alte Kirche—*the old church. I believe that, as we engage in dialogue with it, the old church can help us, even in post-Christendom, to be followers of Jesus Christ in a church that is perennially young.*[1]

....

---

[1] Reprinted by permission of the publisher from Alan Kreider, "Worship and Evangelism in Pre-Christendom" (The Laing Lecture, 1994), *Vox Evangelica* 24 (1994): 29–30.

⋮ J. Nelson Kraybill

Early Sunday morning at a church retreat, I made my way to the dining hall for breakfast, and was surprised to see a small boy named Nathan eating alone. Social services had recently removed him from an abusive situation, and he now was fostered by a family from our church. His new parents reported that he ate meals rapidly because food had been snatched away as a form of punishment in his previous home. I set down my breakfast tray across from Nathan, and asked friendly questions to draw him out, without much success. The boy stared resolutely into his cereal bowl, never answering with more than a word or two.

Two hours later, retreat participants gathered for worship, which included the early Christian practice of footwashing. Adults and children sat in a circle several rows deep to sing, pray, and hear teaching. Then servers placed basins and towels at stations outside the ring. While the group sang hymns, those who wanted to could leave the circle to wash feet in pairs.

Nathan remained on the floor in the center of the circle with other children, but strained to see what was happening at the basins. After returning from my own footwashing, I leaned down and asked Nathan if he wanted to go to see what others were doing. He nodded, and we moved together to sit on the floor near a basin. "We are followers of Jesus," I whispered. "Jesus loved everybody, even people nobody else loved. One of the ways he showed that was by washing their feet." I explained about sandals, dusty roads, and servants washing the feet of guests in the ancient world. Then I asked Nathan if I could wash his feet. He hesitated, then nodded.

The lad was eight and small for his age, with legs that did not reach from chair seat to basin. But I got his feet washed, and he giggled momentarily when I dried his toes. It is customary in our church to hug after footwashing. But Nathan spent years around abusive adults, and did not yet have reason to trust me. So I put my hand on his shoulder, said how glad I was that he was there, and started back to my seat.

But then I felt a tug at my sleeve, and I turned to see Nathan. "I want to wash *your* feet," he whispered urgently. Now it was my turn to pause; in our church tradition nobody gets washed twice. But deeper wisdom prevailed, and I told Nathan that I would love to have him do that for me. I sat down at a basin, removed my shoes, and was washed a second time.

Christians in positions of power

Footwashing was a mundane necessity in ancient Palestine, but Jesus vested it with meaning that overturned conventional power relationships. Now the humble ritual had leapfrogged millennia to connect deeply with me and with a wounded child. But was this connection a fluke? How much ancient Christian liturgical and lifestyle freight can we haul across the centuries, especially when Christianity so often has been co-opted by powerbrokers in government, church, and military?

Nathan knew nothing about Christendom, about the seventeen centuries of alliance between power structures of Western society and followers of the Lamb. But my own path of ministry—from urban schoolteacher in Puerto Rico to seminary president in the United States to pastor—convinced me that the "grand edifice" of Christendom, while diminished, is not gone. I have taught school for upwardly mobile Christian families, have helped raise millions of dollars for the seminary where I worked, and have received tax benefits as an ordained minister. As a white, middle-class, educated American Christian, I have power.

Mennonites, who once were marginalized Anabaptists in Europe, now often have clout in the United States. Elsewhere in the world, Mennonites and other Christians may be a suffering minority. But here we create our own Christendoms, blending economic, social, and political power to achieve status or build institutions. This makes Mennonites susceptible to a symbiotic relationship between church and state that makes us feel secure.

Many Christians in the West live in tension between the vulnerability modeled by Jesus ("Let them . . . take up their cross and follow me" [Mark 8:34]) and the drive for security and comfort that comes naturally for people with power. Our souls become so anesthetized by consumerism and the drive to control that we cannot feel the liberating tug of the gospel ("The truth will set you free" [John 8:32; NIV]).

Even worship practices or lifestyle commitments of the early churches that once freed believers from servitude to self and sin can lose transforming power when removed from their original context. Footwashing, for example, was lost to ordinary Christians during much of Christendom when it became an elite ceremony for state officials, kings, and archbishops, rather than a humble act of service. House churches evolved into cathedrals, and charity became grandstanding philanthropy. Spiritual shepherds became aristocracy, and communion became eucharistic theater before a largely passive crowd.

Incarnation and the early churches

Because we Christians so easily have our heads turned by political or economic power, we occasionally need to ponder the patterns of church behavior common before followers of Jesus went on Christendom steroids. The literary epicenter of our understanding remains the New Testament, especially the teaching of Jesus. At the core of our faith is divine incarnation into a specific historical context. How that singular divine initiative crystallized into the inaugural church community is of paradigmatic importance.

Rich and poor sat at table together and broke bread. People with options for upward mobility chose instead to lay down power and take up a cross. Lepers, immigrants, and urban people in poverty found a place to belong. Worship and catechism in the New Testament churches were exercises of recalibrating allegiance. Liturgy and ritual (such as the laying on of hands to authorize leaders, or exorcism) and new folkways (such as love feasts or intercontinental sharing of money among churches) oriented followers of Jesus toward the new Jerusalem rather than Babylon.

In the fourth century, Christians gained respectability and influence in the Roman Empire—a startling rise to power that profoundly shaped European (and later, North American) society. With access to power comes responsibility and risk. It is easy for modern Christians in this situation to individualize or spiritualize our faith so that the scandal of the cross does not complicate our political and social objectives. It is hard to hear Jesus' call to not store up treasures on earth (Matt. 6:19) when we are key players in a capitalist society.

Actual practice of the early churches

There is reason to believe that Christians in the first centuries actually followed the unsettling behaviors modeled and taught by Jesus, including at least some instances of footwashing.[2] But from fourth- and fifth-century voices we get a sense of what happened with the transition into Christendom. In reference to footwashing, John Chrysostom (ca. 347–407) lamented that he and contemporaries "do not imitate it even slightly," but "on the contrary, adopt the opposite attitude: both magnifying ourselves unduly and not rendering to others what we ought."[3]

Augustine (354–430) recognized that the practice of footwashing had been spiritualized by some believers: "What they do not with the hand they do with the heart." While spiritualized footwashing may have merit, Augustine said, "it is far better, and beyond all dispute more accordant with the truth, that it should also be done with the hands." When the body "is bent at a [saint's] feet," the feeling of humility "is either awakened in the heart itself, or is strengthened if already present."[4]

Why did some pre-Christendom churches actually do footwashing, and why did the practice become spiritualized or nearly

---

[2] Evidence for the actual practice of footwashing in the early church is not abundant, but it is there: John 13:2–17; 1 Tim. 5:10; Tertullian, *De Corona* 8 (ca. 211); Athanasius, *Canons* 66 (ca. 366–73); *Apostolic Constitutions*, 3.19 (late fourth century). See John Christopher Thomas, *Footwashing in John 13 and the Johannine Community* (Sheffield: Sheffield Academic Press, 1991), 127–46.

[3] John Chrysostom, Homily 71 (John 13:12–19), from "Chrysostom's *Commentary on Saint John the Apostle and Evangelist*," trans. Sister Thomas Aquinas Goggin, in *Homilies 48–88* (New York: Fathers of the Church, Inc., 1960), 261.

[4] Augustine, Tractate 59, *Homilies on the Gospel of John*, trans. John Gibb and James Innes, in *Nicene and Post-Nicene Fathers* 8, ed. Philip Schaff (Grand Rapids, MI: Eerdmans, 1974), 306.

extinct as Christendom emerged? If we do not grasp something of the sociological and historical context in which the early churches took root, we might not understand why the gospel was both life-giving and offensive. If we do not understand how beliefs and practices got refracted by the ascent of the church to political sovereignty, we might not be alert to the ways our own affiliation with power alters the gospel. We might not have eyes to see how the message of Jesus should be confronting us and our culture today.

The cross, for example, now often serves as jewelry or as a mere token of personal piety. We could learn from the early churches that the cross represented costly confrontation with political and spiritual powers, that it was such a ghastly instrument of death that no Christians even displayed the symbol before the fourth century.[5] We could still hold high the cross, but it may radicalize us.

Basic human impulses remain unchanged

With imagination and scholarly tools, we can traverse the hump of history between the early churches and the twenty-first century. Basic human impulses of greed, lust, and violence have changed little in two thousand years. Empire remains empire, whether emanating from Rome, Washington, or multinational corporations. Wealth and luxury make us salivate just as they did Cyprian of Carthage.[6]

We must not be naive about pre-Christendom, however, imagining that all early believers got faith practices right or heroically suffered at the margins of society. The early churches were diverse, and rife with conflict about theology and praxis. Some early Christians were wealthy, educated, and from privileged backgrounds. But we can learn from them, especially how they formed alternative communities at a time when wider society gave them little respect or access to conventional power. The early churches were the first sustained practical experiments of the kingdom of God as proclaimed by Jesus, and early believers embodied the faith in a world

---

[5] Graydon F. Snyder, *Ante Pacem: Archaeological Evidence of Church Life before Constantine*, rev. ed. (Macon, GA: Mercer University Press, 2003), 58–64.

[6] Cyprian, *Epistle* 1, *Ad Donatum* 3–4.

as diverse and violent as ours. Especially when critics today cata-
logue the moral failures of Christendom, we need the sheer inspiration value of pre-Christendom stories and insights.

Alan and Eleanor Kreider have explored early Christian practices from communion to catechesis to mission. Eucharist, they
point out, involved sharing material resources and restoring broken
relationships. Catechesis included comprehensive review of lifestyle
and ethics. Mission entailed being ready to explain why believers
behaved oddly. Throughout this teaching is an underlying theme:
early Christians understood themselves to be part of an alternative community, a distinct and demanding allegiance, a kingdom
citizenship, a new humanity. It is from this sense of being a people
apart—yet engaged in the world—that today's believers have the
most to learn from the early churches.

Whom will we obey?

Recently a man at my neighborhood gym wore a T-shirt with a
large design that looked like the Burger King logo—except instead
of reading "Burger King" the logo said "Christ is King." After
receiving enthusiastic permission to ask a question about his attire,
I posed a dilemma: if the president of the United States said you
should put on a uniform and kill, and Christ said you should love
your enemies, whom would you obey?

Invoking the submit-to-governing-authorities teaching of Paul
(Rom. 13), my Christian friend said he would kill. So in the hard
circumstances of conflict, I ventured, Christ is not really king, the
president is. No, Christ is king, he insisted; the important thing is
that we *know* him. I suggested that there were many people who
knew Jesus, but that did not bring them into the kingdom. Jesus
blessed those who not only hear the word but obey it (Luke 11:28).

Percolating under my impertinence was the witness of the early churches—especially instructions for catechism in the *Apostolic
Tradition* from the church at Rome (ca. 200). In those pre-Christendom days, if a candidate for baptism already was in the army, the

church required him not to kill. Candidates who joined the army after making a confession of faith could not receive baptism.[7]

My gym companion was not interested in the early churches, and he returned to weightlifting. He and I live in a society that is morphing from Christendom into pluralism and neopaganism. Both of us take the Bible seriously, and both want to be faithful to Jesus. Inspiration from the early churches, from before Christianity was seduced by its own political success, could give both of us muscle for bearing subversive and life-giving good news.

: Mark Van Steenwyk

For the past several years, I've had the privilege of connecting with emerging radical communities and intentional communities from Seattle to New York, from Winnipeg to Mexico City. As I travel to connect with these pockets of radical Christianity, I am convinced of something: America desperately needs the Anabaptist witness. Individuals and groups are discovering within the gospel a message that Anabaptists have held for half a millennium. Sadly, while new communities are forming that hold values strikingly compatible with Anabaptist values, many Mennonites seem to be giving up traditional Anabaptist convictions.

This isn't just speculation from a Mennonite insider; my community and I have only been officially Mennonite for two years. In fact, there is only one person in our congregation who comes from a Mennonite background. But we are deeply drawn to the peculiarities of Anabaptism. By naming Christendom as a detriment to faith, Anabaptists are uniquely situated to embrace some of the more marginal voices from the early Christian movement. We also, I believe, have an amazing opportunity to anticipate the future.

All around the world, people are rising up to challenge the predominant "isms" of our day—consumerism, militarism, individualism, among others. These things, woven together, form the fabric

---

[7] Alan Kreider, *The Change of Conversion and the Origin of Christendom* (Harrisburg, PA: Trinity Press International, 1999), 23.

of a sort of secular Western paganism—a pseudospirituality into which most of the West is baptized. A new generation is beginning to question the imperial posture of the United States, to question the healthiness of consumer culture, and to look for healthy alternative ways of life. Christians and non-Christians are waking from the American Dream.

So now, more than ever, we need to boldly embrace being, as Alan Kreider suggests, "known as members of a *superstitio*, a deviation from the norms of accepted behavior." In the shadow of militarism, we can be peacemakers. In a land of consumerism, we can live simply. Instead of living individualistically, we can be a hospitable community.

This growing movement of kingdom counterculturality has much in common with the Anabaptist tradition, but it is emerging from outside that tradition. The challenge is clear: we can either shrink back from our distinctiveness or join with this growing movement in celebrating our peculiarity. We can either bury our most radical convictions or risk our stability and safety to be a part of the subversive thing that the Spirit is stirring.

Kyong-Jung Kim

Alan and Eleanor Kreider were our first guest speakers at the Korea Anabaptist Center in 2003. At that time KAC was still new to the Korean church and society. Most Korean churches' top priorities were evangelism and church planting. As a result, there are thousands of churches almost everywhere in South Korea. It seemed Korean Christianity was ever growing. If we could keep bringing people from outside, converting them to Christianity, and sending missionaries, churches should have been full of joy and celebration all the time.

But in reality, churches often struggle with conflicts, tensions, and even broken relationships, which lead at times to internal splits. No wonder that the Korean church has stopped growing in number and receives criticism in many areas of social life. What does this mean to us today? The early church stories the Kreiders brought had significant implications for the Korean church situation.

A traditional view of church growth was changed from a focus on mass evangelism to personal relationship building. Even though quite a number of churches still work hard on numerical church growth, some other churches (usually small ones) work really hard on fostering genuine relationships between believers and nonbelievers. One example happened in the city of Busan, South Korea.

A Presbyterian church there rebaptized all its members, including the head pastor, to renew their church membership. This was done after the Kreiders' teaching about the early church's perspective on baptism and its process for inducting new members. In the same town a Baptist church experienced a significant loss in membership because they applied to their congregation an understanding of membership drawn from an early church perspective. These two churches plus other individuals were quite happy to receive the Kreiders' words. Their fellowship surpassed their denominational background, joyfully meeting in a shared place of common understanding that was provided by Anabaptist scholars. It seems that these Anabaptists were strengthening the relationship between these two Korean (Presbyterian and Baptist) churches but also helping them walk in the paths of the early church. This was how the Kreiders' teaching had an impact on two Korean churches.

The Kreiders' perspective on the growth of the early church showed how different it was: there was no evangelism program like we have today, but its worship was intriguingly attractive, and the Christian way of life was different from that of outsiders. The Kreiders challenged our typical understandings of worship, membership, discipleship, and our relationship to others. They provided Korean audiences with a new window through which to look at how the church of Christ in all ages should function.

The Kreiders' input paved the road for the Korea Anabaptist Center to be engaged in further dialogue with Korean churches about genuine faith and life issues from an Anabaptist perspective, which was along the same lines as the early church. Starting with the Kreiders, the KAC has received Anabaptist speakers, including Nelson Kraybill, every year. Whenever they have shared their stories and gospel messages, I have felt that different pieces of the puzzle that make up the whole picture of God's kingdom were being put together. Thank God for sending Jesus Christ to be a perfect example for all churches to follow.

IV.
Worship

12

Prayer
Imagine a new world

Dare to be a Mary . . . In using scripture in worship, do we have the privilege of editing the scripture? Within certain limits, yes, we do. It is essential that we give careful thought and detailed work to the process of preparing scripture readings for worship. It is important to have a stated and shared understanding within the congregation about this process. Clarity, faithfulness to the meanings, and communication are criteria for the work.

In making selections and being careful in the public presentation of scripture, we are following in the tradition of the writers and compilers of the Bible. We are also following Christian liturgists and devotional writers through the ages.

Mary, the mother of Jesus, was an editor as well as a poet. As a child, she had memorized scripture. Passages from the Law, the Psalms, and the Prophets were deeply and safely stored in her mind. The angel's words, "You have found favor with God," struck her with fear and awe. Terrified and inspired, Mary poured out her psalm of enlivened nuggets of scripture (Hab. 3:18; Job 5:11; 2 Sam. 22:28; parts of Psalms 34, 35, 89, 98, 103, 107, 111, 147).

Out the Bible phrases flowed, connected in a new way. In her devout response, Mary spoke out new scripture. The Magnificat was not original; it was all rooted in the longings, the faith, the agonies, and the hopes expressed in the Hebrew scriptures Mary knew so well.

But at the same time the Magnificat was new. It was new because Mary's experience and the words of scripture joined to produce a poetic prayer unlike any other before it. It was more than the sum of its parts, as a baked custard is different from the individual components—the eggs, the sugar, and the milk.

Jesus, too, was a poet. He was an editor as well as a prophet. Steeped in scripture as his mother before him was, he met life and its crises with the potent forces of scripture, Spirit, insight, and image. Jesus' manifesto in Luke 4 is edited from Isaiah (chapters 61 and 58). The Great Commandment is edited from the Law (Deut. 6:5; Lev. 19:18). Jesus often built his poetic parables on older rabbinic stories. The turns of phrase, the sharp insights, were his Spirit-inspired genius at work, bringing life and scripture together in homely and vivid ways.

We are not going to write new scripture. We are not Mary or Jesus. But we can follow in their steps by saturating our minds with scripture. We, like them, can allow scripture to be, in fresh ways, a smoothed path for public worship. When we don't know the words to use, one of the ways the Spirit provides for our prayers is through Bible words . . .

Praying in our own words, extempore, is good. But we must be careful not to fall into habits of using worn-out or debased words. The best way to avoid getting into ruts and repetitions is to feed our minds on Bible words. The Bible will give strong structure and sensible meaning to our prayers. Preparing public prayers for church services isn't easy. It requires gift, imagination, and a strong commitment of time and mental energy. But when we are willing to grow and change, how fruitful the results can be . . .

"Bless those who curse you; pray for those who mistreat you" (Luke 6:28). Jesus can't be serious! How can we pray for those who malign our friends, who torture and imprison Christians, who dismiss our convictions and ridicule our faith? We feel unable to do anything more than look on in stupefied horror and complain bitterly to each other. Above all, we learn to be practical and keep our own heads down, out of danger.

But Jesus was truly practical and realistic. He knew the heart of his Abba, and he had the clear eye of the prophet. Jesus recalled Jeremiah, prophet to sixth-century BC Hebrews. Jeremiah was living in Jerusalem just before Babylon, the national enemy, burned the city and took its residents into captivity. His advice was eloquent, practical, and humane. He spoke in the name of the Lord God of Israel, because he understood God's vision of justice and peace among the nations.

"Seek the welfare of the city where I have sent you into exile. Pray to the Lord on its behalf, for in its welfare you will find your welfare" (Jer. 29:7; RSV).

We live in a world possessed. We see the grip of evil forces over neighbors and ourselves. In the communal violence of such places as Ulster, South Africa, or Central America, these forces of evil openly display their frightening grip. But many aspects of our own corporate lives are also influenced by evil forces that are unseen or unrecognized.

The effect of Christ's victory over the powers of death is vastly greater than we know or can imagine. In Colossians 2:15, we read that on the cross Jesus "disarmed the powers and authorities; he made a public spectacle of them, triumphing over them."

We can't comprehend the full meaning of this victory. Yet we sense the truth of the allusion to forces beyond our sight which have great control in our society. Christians require courageous determination to oppose contemporary idolatry. These struggles call on the prayer power of the church.

Scales must fall from our eyes so that we see how to pray for the churches and for others in places of conflict. We are not helpless. We are responsible to love our neighbors, our brothers and sisters, and our enemies. We combat the powers of darkness in the name of Jesus the victor. Intercession is the work of the church.[1]

....

: Sian Murray Williams

I have a childhood memory of standing in a group of children at the front of Bethania Baptist Chapel in West Wales, reciting in turn a Bible verse learned in the previous week. This regular pattern of sharing verses was simply part of life. It was about learning the Bible by heart so that these verses neatly embedded in a deep mine of faith could be called on to give comfort, challenge, affirmation,

---

[1] Reprinted from *Enter His Gates: Fitting Worship Together*, by Eleanor Kreider. Copyright © 1990 by Herald Press, Scottdale PA 15683. Used by permission.

and direction in life. Today, there are no children in that church, but the aging congregation keeps the tradition alive through finding and learning verses of scripture that resonate with the theme of the upcoming Sunday's service. This is not a tale of profound tussling with scripture, but it speaks of a rhythm of engaging with the text so that the people of God in the act of choosing the text make connections between it, life, and worship.

God's people are called to robust engagement with the scriptures

Whatever happened to learning by heart? A few years ago a *Baptist Times* article carried news of a survey that suggested that about 75 percent of people sitting in Baptist churches in the UK do not read their Bibles from one Sunday to the next. Their only hearing and reading of the text comes within corporate Sunday worship.

Alarm bells ring. What story are we handing on to our children? What does our lack of engagement with the Bible say about how we view God? How are the stories and poems, the legal codes and prophecies, the visions and letters forming us more closely into the likeness of Christ? How do the ancient stories of faith help us in our understanding of God, our following of Jesus, our being enlivened by the Spirit? How does the poetry and imagery of the Bible inform our speaking with God?

Mary is able to call on the scriptures, drawing on rich language—the only language possible—to express her delight at God's activity in the Incarnation. Jesus incorporates scripture into daily conversation, where the text and context dovetail to create a startling opportunity for new truth to be known.

We are called to a robust engagement with the unique resource gifted to us. And why? As James McClendon asserts,

> Whenever it speaks, its story not only supports and conserves, but challenges and corrects and sometimes flatly defeats the tales we tell ourselves about ourselves. God's Spirit who breathed upon the writers of the Scriptures breathes also on us, sometimes harshly. The consequence is that our stubborn wills are turned, our blind eyes opened, our arrhythmic hearts

set beating in tempo. This is not always immediate and is never without ugly exceptions; but it happens often enough to confirm our faith in the Author of the Book.[2]

Scripture helps us dream. We need scripture to enlarge our imagination and to expand our faith, as time and time again we get to exclaim—See! See what happened here and what God has done! Scripture gives us permission to dream daringly about a new heaven and a new earth. It is soaked in images to help us do just that. What is the kingdom of God like? It is like this. It is like that. And where is the kingdom of God? It is here. It is there. Come and see!

Scripture connects us to the broader faith family. Scripture rehearses the stories of men and women who have faced exactly the same questions that we face, although in a multitude of different contexts. Through the differences comes a piercing light that illuminates the truth about our shared humanity. We recognize them. They live halfway round the world. They are next door. They are family. They are us.

Scripture shapes our prayer life. Scripture nourishes our imagination and informs our prayer, the two feeding from each other to break new realities into our consciousness, to make new things possible, to enable a more faithful following. When this vast landscape of shattering images and audacious language meets our deepest hopes and fears, we are in the realm of dangerous, risky, and subversive prayer.

From bored intonation to passionate realignment with God's purposes

Now, this description might not seem a good fit with our most recent experience of corporate prayer when we last met with the people of God. All too often, our bored intonation, our lowest-common-denominator use of language, our lack of expectation of divine encounter, our failure in anticipating newness, can easily lead us to a life of prayer as rote without riot. Controlled and controlling, we

---

[2] J. W. McClendon, *Systematic Theology: Doctrine* (Nashville, TN: Abingdon Press, 1994), 41.

can forget the prophetic passion and robust rudeness of the psalmist; we can avoid Hezekiah's poured-out grief; we can domesticate Hannah and Mary's overwhelming joy at the stripping of the powers of death; we can reduce David's confessional angst to a jaunty tune; and we can pacify Jesus' volcanic yearning for justice. Prayer that does not open up within us the possibility of unsettling percolation is not found in scripture.

Prayer has been described as "aligning our will with the will of God."[3] This is not a gentle activity. While contemplation and meditation involve the inhabiting of quiet, undistracted space, realignment calls for struggle as we move from egocentrism to a rootedness in God, our rock and redeemer. All forms of prayer lead us in this direction, expanding within us a vision of God, humanity, and creation. All forms of prayer strip from us the illusory buttresses we use to sustain false images of reality. All forms of prayer confront us with light and truth. They become the way in which the life of the one who is the truth, the way, and the life is grown within us. All forms of prayer involve a giving up and a taking up. To pretend otherwise is simply foolish.

How then should this ravaging and redemptive activity be known among us? Oh, that as much preparation and forethought went into the prayers we pray in communities of faith as goes into the sermon or music practice! There is a rich tradition of extempore prayer among believers church communities. The shape of that extempore prayer has been explored in two key ways.

Fostering extempore prayer in corporate worship

First, the one responsible for leading the people in prayer has been immersed in the text from which the word will be preached, and in the context in which the people have found themselves during that week or that season. That immersion should result in public prayer in which the rhythms of language, theme, and application can find their way into a form of words addressed to God that elicit a sometimes wholehearted, often trembling "Amen!" from the people.

---

[3] This quotation is sometimes attributed to Methodist missionary E. Stanley Jones.

Second, the one with that responsibility is inspired to pray in the moment, "as the Spirit leads." What guides this prayer is a listening ear and a heart attuned to the movement of God in the company of the people, a concerned and compassionate awareness of the life of the world, and a commitment to a God-given vision for all creation. This attentiveness releases the voice to pray with passion, understanding, and arrant boldness.

And in the traditions that have prayerfully worked with the language of prayer, honing it and crafting it to be beautiful and powerful, we can see at work dangerous phrases spoken out to God. Annie Dillard sums it up beautifully: "I often think of the set pieces of liturgy as certain words that people have successfully addressed to God without their getting killed."[+]

Whichever way we prefer the form, prayer is a risky place in which to find ourselves. But finding ourselves there is exactly what will happen when we follow Jesus. His call to follow was not offered as some form of palliative for a troubled soul. It is a call to follow into fullness of life, of wholeness and wholehearted engagement with a troubled world. Eleanor Kreider speaks of prayer as work. She is right. It is a part of the priestly calling of the church to work for the shalom of all creation.

Imagine what would happen if . . .

Imagine what would happen if churches who struggle to find their true identity in a rapidly changing culture prayed impassioned prayers to God. We would have a community of faith able to offer its struggle to be relevant on the one hand and countercultural on the other, yearning for the sight to see the world as it could be, and calling its people to prayerful engagement with that change. We would have a community of faith begging God for the ability to discern between the cultural voices that clamor for attention and the voice of God calling the people to faithful, radical, and just living.

For the corporate prayer of the church is about reorienting the world just that little bit more so that all parts of creation are

[+] Annie Dillard, "Holy the Firm," in *The Annie Dillard Reader* (New York: Harper Collins, 1995), 447.

enabled, in God's mercy, to fulfill their purpose. The prayer of the church is about mending the brokenness of nature and communities. It's about confounding the purposes of those who would seek to profit from disaster and oppress the poor. It's about crying out a deep desire for the world's systems and people to be liberated from greed, to live in peace, prospering in all that they do. It's a radical standing with those who have lost their voice in a fog of despair. It's a brazen holding of a fragmented world before its Creator saying, "This will not do!" Prayer is an act of spiritual defiance, says Walter Wink, and in a short sentence offers the huge scope of such defiant prayer: "History belongs to the intercessors who believe the future into being."[5]

The act of prayer is a place of encounter and change. And the prayers that we pray do not begin in our hearts. As we align our will with the will of God, we learn that the prayers we pray, the cries we shout aloud, the deepest yearnings of our hearts, however imperfectly expressed, have their source in the heart of God. It is in prayer that we know and feel the passion of the Trinity. The most ardent prayers we pray for the coming kingdom are but a fraction of the desire known by God.

The mystery is, of course, how we are ourselves changed through the prayers we pray. The God of all mercy works with us through them to restore, resurrect, and redeem the broken places and darkened corners of a battered world. The cross of Christ and his resurrection have done the work. Creation is being redeemed. The new community of Christ is commissioned with the work of proclaiming and practicing that redemptive work in embodied ways, incarnating new hope and a new future.

Impassioned prayer and the ushering in of a brand new world? *Just imagine . . .*

---

[5] Walter Wink, *Engaging the Powers: Discernment and Resistance in a World of Domination* (Minneapolis: Augsburg Press, 1999), 299.

⠂ Gene Herr

The words of Eleanor Kreider and Sian Murray Williams speak of the interrelationship of scripture, worship, and mission. Sian, out of her childhood in Wales, and Eleanor, from her leadership at the London Mennonite Centre, Prairie Street Mennonite Church in Elkhart, Indiana, and other places, call us to be transformed into servants for the renewal of individuals, their gathered life, and the earth.

To make something real, make it local.

Eleanor and Alan have embodied this reality in the hospitality of their Elkhart home, "The Eighth Day." The creativity of this home is signified by the hug at the door and the room set apart for group prayer with hymnals and copies of *Take Our Moments and Our Days*—an Anabaptist prayer book—available and ready for use.[6]

A comment about a neighbor whose need is on the Kreiders' heart may slip into the exchange during tea. The house is located so they can and *do* walk to the three foci of their lives in Elkhart—the seminary, the church, and the home of their son Andrew and his family. The Kreiders' writing and team teaching come out of healed and healing meditation, intercession, and available servanthood.

My yes to the Kreider and Williams pieces comes in this form. Both the incarnate Word and that which is written are only perceived by revelation (Matt. 16:17; Eph. 1:17). Jesus spoke of hearing and understanding, seeing and perceiving (Matt. 13:14). In 1 Corinthians 2:6-16, Paul enlarges on the Spirit's work of opening ears, eyes, and heart. Our research in scripture and history demands attentiveness as well as inquisitiveness. We are prayed as we pray (Rom. 8:26).

When I was a college student in the early 1950s, a visiting pastor taught us the gift of the prayers of Paul. Special focus was on Ephesians 1:15–23 and 3:14–21, Colossians 1:9–14, Philippians 1:9–11, and 2 Thessalonians 1:11–12. These prayers have formed

---

[6] Arthur Paul Boers, Barbara Nelson Gingerich, Eleanor Kreider, John Rempel, and Mary H. Schertz, *Take Our Moments and Our Days: An Anabaptist Prayer Book*, vol. 1: *Ordinary Time* (Scottdale, PA: Herald Press, 2007).

my intercessions on many occasions, both for myself and for those whom I have sought to companion. Paul envisioned a people vibrant, deep, and whole. And so can we!

My wife, Mary, and I attended Mennonite World Conference in Asuncíon, Paraguay, in July 2009. On my return, while preparing a report to our local church, I thought of the incongruities of my two experiences. In Paraguay we met with a vast array of Mennonite groups from scores of countries, while in the small town of Hesston, Kansas, local churches gather in isolation from one another. I prepared a proposal to suggest that our local congregation might give leadership to an intercongregational gathering. I also found some ways to pray and worship with a pastor and two of the congregations. Jesus' prayers will demand intentional obedience.

While leading congregational prayer recently, I felt I had to bring into the intercessions the other congregations within a ten-mile radius and pray for God's blessings and wisdom for them by name. For me, the final prayer of Jesus with the disciples recorded in John 17 is tied to Eleanor's reference to "seeking the welfare of the city to which we are sent."

The core biblical text for the Mennonite Assembly in Paraguay (2009) was Philippians 2:5–11. The prior context in verses 3 and 4 of chapter 2 is this instruction: "In humility value others above yourselves, not looking to your own interests but each of you to the interests of others" (NIV). We seek the welfare of other disciple entities as well as our own.

While pastoring in a small rural community in south-central Kansas some years ago, I safeguarded against "my/our" church being my only focus by kneeling each week with another pastor for a blessing on him and his ministry. As local pastors in that town, we each agreed to pray for the other's congregation whenever we drove by its place of worship. That little town had a wide variety of denominational biases, but we sought to pray and bless one another. And we did. People felt that something new was happening.

For several years I was part of a homeless shelter team envisioning and experiencing a wondrous availability to serve those with temporary needs for food, shelter, and companioning in discerning next steps. The prayer of John 17 is made local and visible.

⦂ Neal and Janie Blough

For many years now, we have benefited from the careful work of Alan and Eleanor Kreider, especially the insights offered in Eleanor's *Enter His Gates* and Alan's work on the early church. Relationships with the Kreiders have put a new face on worship and inspired Janie to begin her own walk into that world. Their enthusiasm, biblical scholarship, and pastoral hearts have also encouraged her to be a constant and patient advocate for the use of more scripture in worship and in the prayer life of the church.

After more than thirty years of worshiping in two multicultural urban Mennonite congregations, we are struck by how the cross-cultural, transcultural, and countercultural reality reflected in one tiny microcosm of the world church can nourish the prayer life of a community by literally bringing the world to the minds of those praying. We can think of many examples that have helped us imagine God's new world during Sunday morning intercessory prayer: a Congolese brother who learned that his father in Eastern Congo was supposedly dead, and then six months later discovered that he was in fact alive; a sister from Cameroon reporting on a brother who is in jail on false pretenses; women from Congo constantly reminding us of the horrors taking place in the Great Lakes region; an "illegal" immigrant woman seeking papers, a home, and a job in Paris; a pastor's Ukrainian wife requesting prayer for recent elections; the pain of Haitian families trying to come to grips with the death and destruction of a recent earthquake in their country.

Words from scripture and rootedness in the Gospel narrative nourish our prayer life, but so do encounters with "real" people dealing with harsh situations of suffering and war. The reality of situations of such intolerable injustice shakes us out of our comfy complacency and reminds us that peace and justice are more than theological concepts. The many faces of the church gathered together in one community can be a stimulus to prayer.

But what if a congregation is more homogeneous, composed primarily of members from one cultural reality? The prayer life of local churches can still be enriched by the global church. Global tunes, stories, exchanges, and an awareness of the economic, social, and political realities of our brothers and sisters in the international church, especially in the global South, can bring fresh perspectives and global concerns that can and should nourish our prayer lives.

To paraphrase Walter Wink, history belongs to the intercessors who pray God's past and God's future into the global present.[7]

---

[7] See n5 above.

13

Communion
Renew the covenant

In the Eucharist, the risen Christ meets his people and feeds them, shaping them into the forgiven and forgiving body of Christ. As they eat and drink, the people are filled with thanksgiving and go out with joy.

During the Christendom centuries this joyful communal thanksgiving was not always evident. Screens and fences separated priests from the people, and the priests spoke in a language that few people could understand. The Liturgical Movement of the twentieth century did much to restore to many churches the sense that the people participate fully in the mnemonic meal along with the presiding clerics, though many people still feel that the laity are bit-part players on the margins of the drama of the Lord's Supper. Nevertheless, at its heart the Eucharist remains a sacrament of God's mission.

- *The Eucharist tells the story of God. It is the narrative sacrament par excellence. In it, the worshipers celebrate the coming together of past, present, and future. They recollect, they celebrate, and they longingly anticipate. By ritually playing this meal, the participants enter into it and become participants in the life, death, resurrection, and reign of Christ. By eating and drinking together, and by making peace with one another, they also are re-membered as his body.[1]*

- *The Eucharist commits the worshipers to participate in God's mission. It is a renewal of the new covenant. In it, the believers, in the presence of Christ their host, renew their commitment to the "new covenant in his blood." As they do so, they enter into his mission*

---

[1] William Cavanaugh, *Torture and Eucharist* (Oxford: Blackwell, 1998), 229.

and his politics. "The regular renewal of the covenant means that the people of God are constantly confirmed in and impelled to mission."[2] Through the Eucharist, Christ reconciles his disciples to God and makes them ministers of reconciliation to their neighbors and enemies. Anabaptist theologian Balthasar Hubmaier expressed this connection—which we have called the "motive clause"—at the conclusion of the communion service which he wrote shortly before his martyrdom in 1528: "As Christ gave up his life for me, so I go forth to give up my life for others, for my sisters and brothers in faith, my neighbors, my enemies."[3] In the safer world of the 1960s, J. G. Davies also saw this connection. "Authentic worship," he wrote,[4] is "that in which the two dimensions are combined, viz. participation in Christ through communion and so participation in his mission to the world."

In the "classic" approach to communion, outsiders were admitted only after baptism. Pre-Christendom churches as early as the one addressed in the Didache forbade unbaptized outsiders to take part in the Eucharist. And from the second century, only the baptized could be present at the Eucharist. So it has continued as Christendom developed in the fourth century and across the history of Christianity both Western and Eastern: baptism has been a prerequisite for participation in communion—unbaptized outsiders have often been excluded from observing it.

This tradition has had great strengths. It has rooted its practice in the assumption that Jesus participated in two sorts of meals: meals of radical openness with all sorts of people, including "tax collectors and sinners"; and meals of radical intentionality with Jesus' inner circle (of which the Last Supper is paradigmatic), in which his disciples express willingness to join Jesus in "drinking the cup" (Mark 10:38; Luke 22:15). For the church, baptism in which one dies to an old life has come to be the necessary precondition for participation in the meals of Jesus' kingdom life; for the

---

[2] J. G. Davies, *Worship and Mission* (London: SCM Press, 1966), 94.

[3] Balthasar Hubmaier, "Form for Christ's Supper" (1527), in *Balthasar Hubmaier: Theologian of Anabaptism*, ed. H. Wayne Pipkin and John H. Yoder (Scottdale, PA: Herald Press, 1989), 404.

[4] Davies, *Worship and Mission*, 98.

kingdom meals empower Jesus' disciples to live the life of sacrificial self-giving which expresses itself in radical hospitality.

Some people today view boundaries as unwelcoming, but adherents of this position observe that welcome is genuine only when it is welcome to a community that unabashedly stands for something and whose members have sacrificed in order to join it. Boundaries can be hospitable. Furthermore, boundaried communities can be missionally alert; they can issue a genuine invitation, not just to casual participation, but to covenant in baptism which leads to the feast of the new covenant. Until the outsiders are catechized and baptized, they will engage in the countercultural discipline of longing which, at the right moment, will be joyously satisfied at the Eucharistic table.

This boundaried approach has been dominant in the West. In this, members of the Anabaptist tradition have agreed with Christians in the great Christendom traditions—outsiders should not be served at the communion table.[5] We believe that, where this tradition is functioning at its best, it can be missional and attract outsiders in post-Christendom. Baptism is the pathway to the Eucharist.

However, we offer four cautions to churches that maintain this classic, "bounded set" approach. First, these churches must emphasize the significance of baptism. Their Eucharists are open only to those who have submitted themselves to the way and cup of Jesus in baptism; so for many Christian traditions, the bounded set position requires baptismal renewal—the baptism of catechized believers, or at least the baptism of children of parents who commit themselves to raising their children as disciples of Jesus who, at the right time, will be intensively catechized. Second, bounded set churches must bless the outsiders. In Eucharists in which the community's boundaries withhold the bread and wine from the outsiders, those presiding at the Eucharists must issue a warm invitation to the outsiders to nonroutine, ritually rich blessings. They may also invite them to faith in Jesus Christ, culminating in baptism and discipleship.

Third, bounded set churches must be churches of many tables. If a church reserves its eucharistic table to baptized believers, it must offer many other meals in which it demonstrates that it knows that Jesus practiced radical

[5] John D. Rempel, *The Lord's Supper in Anabaptism*, Studies in Anabaptist and Mennonite History 33 (Scottdale, PA: Herald Press, 1993), 33–37.

hospitality. A church that does not compress its entire life into an hour on Sunday morning, that has a rich communal life, that greets the outsider with a multidimensional welcome at many tables in a life of fellowship and learning that is open to all—such a church can ask people to wait until they are baptized to participate in the Eucharist. Finally, the bounded set churches' boundaries must not lead communicants to be self-satisfied. Members must not think that only they—the baptized ones—have arrived, smug in their safety within the boundary. Instead the eucharistic meals must empower those who eat and drink to live the intriguing and insecure life of Christ's disciples, moving with him beyond the boundaries toward the outsiders in whom the missio Dei may be at work.[6]

....

⦂ Anne Wilkinson-Hayes

"Oh, by the way," concluded the worship leader at the end of the service I was visiting, "there's communion on the tables at the back—help yourself on your way out . . . if you want." I was stunned, and all the more by the fact that everyone around me seemed to accept this statement as normal. But was it any worse than the service I attended on a freezing cold Christmas Eve in a beautiful twelfth-century building, where the liturgy was pared down to the absolute minimum, conducted at speed and with all the soul of a fast-food outlet, without even the perfunctory "Have a nice day"?

What have we done to the Lord's Supper?

What have we done to the expression of sharing the Lord's Supper that makes it such a pale shadow of the Kreiders' aspiration to "joyful communal thanksgiving"?

I have had good experiences of communion. The church where I was a member in Australia had an unusually rich liturgical life for a Baptist church. The Eucharist was very much the focus and climax of the beautiful liturgy, but the lengthy service was not for the faint-

---

[6] Reprinted from *Worship and Mission after Christendom*, by Alan and Eleanor Kreider. Copyright © 2011 by Herald Press, Scottdale PA 15683. Used by permission.

hearted; it often lasted well over two hours. Occasionally, toward the end of a particularly demanding marathon, I was reminded of one of Alan and Ellie's stories from the London Mennonite Centre. They were enjoying a carefully constructed, thoughtful communion service, and a "gentleman of the road" was shuffling around at the back, becoming more agitated, until he eventually exclaimed, "For God's sake, cut the crap and give us some !@#$% bread!"

Probably my best experiences remain those in my university days—when charismatic renewal was sweeping churches of all theological persuasions. I attended a packed high Anglican church where we all sensed that we were caught up together in a new movement of God. I was joyously swept up to the altar by a passionate singing of the Gloria and softly returned with the strains of "Lamb of God, who takes away the sin of the world . . ." It felt as though something momentous was happening among us—that God was present, and together we were being lovingly shaped for service.

Sadly, that was thirty years ago, and I have participated in or led communion services in hundreds of churches of different denominations since then, and so rarely ever have a similar sense of joyful communal thanksgiving. Why not? And does it matter? Is the sharing of communion essential to a life of committed discipleship? Eleanor believes so. She writes, "Churches will be renewed when the Lord's Supper, graced by God's presence and Word, oriented to the living Lord and empowered by the Spirit, is fully restored to the place that it had in the early centuries—as the central communal Christian act of worship."[7]

Two aspects of communion are required
The Kreiders argue that two aspects of communion are required— to tell the story of God and to celebrate the meal in such a way that it sends the participants out renewed in their commitment to mission. These two characteristics give us some important clues about why so many experiences of sharing in the Lord's Supper are so lacking. A halfhearted ritual tacked onto the end of a service does

---

[7] Eleanor Kreider, *Communion Shapes Character* (Scottdale, PA: Herald Press, 1997), 15.

not give sufficient time either to do justice to the story of God's plan for salvation or for any kind of meaningful response to the event. If we are to celebrate the Lord's Supper with any integrity and import, it needs to be the main event, not an afterthought.

We can work on ways to tell God's story by ensuring an active listening to God's word, the use of visual and other media, and a participatory sharing of stories of God's activities in the lives of people today. But I am intrigued by how celebrating the Lord's Supper can assist in sending God's people out into mission. It is clear that this was a key Anabaptist understanding, and contemporary theologians are seeking to reassert the link. "We would most profoundly misunderstand the Eucharist . . . if we thought of it only as a sacrament of God's embrace of which we are simply the fortunate beneficiaries. Inscribed on the very heart of God's grace is the rule that we can be its recipients only if we do not resist being made into its agents; what happens to us must be done by us."[8]

Making sense of the Eucharist in a post-Christendom era

At my own church the weekly service closes with the words "The Eucharist never ends; it must be lived." But how does what we do around the table help or hinder this living?

One factor in this post-Christendom age might be some false assumptions. Any celebration of communion in an ecclesial setting requires a high degree of imagination on the part of the congregation. The symbols of bread and wine are to be viewed as related to the events of the Last Supper, and as part of a banquet that God lays out for all people—a foretaste of heaven. There is an assumption that people can take that creative leap and make positive associations with communal meals around a table. In an era when few people own a table, and most meals are taken individually or consumed watching the TV, there is a growing gap in what clergy assume is in people's minds and what might actually be there. In addition there is a further assumption of some bucolic association with family meals, when in reality such occasions are often full of tensions

---

[8] Miroslav Volf, *Exclusion and Embrace: A Theological Exploration of Identity, Otherness and Reconciliation* (Nashville, TN: Abingdon Press, 1996), 129.

and endured rather than enjoyed. Increasingly, the ritual event is becoming less and less something that makes sense to contemporary imaginations, so it is hardly surprising that people may not miss occasionally partaking of a thimble of sweet pink water or an anemic cube of white bread or a weird little wafer.

One response is reintroducing the sharing of bread and wine in the context of a normal family meal as an expression of mission. A number of us have experimented with this over many years. When the Kreiders were in Oxford, they joined with us in "Group" — an informal weekly gathering that was generally a joyful communal thanksgiving that enabled many of us to maintain our energy for mission in other places. In Australia we extended this concept, alongside another couple who had been badly burnt in church life and had largely given up any formal church attendance. Over the years we gathered many such people, including several who had never had any faith experience. At "Tablechurch" they found a place where they could share life and explore faith honestly, and do so in the context of a common meal. Tables often had to be extended, but we have kept the discipline of sitting around one table—however squashed that might make things. Children have had a key role in the evenings, and we have experimented with different ways of telling God's story. The group has listened and held people in their pain, and together we have witnessed many life transformations. In my heart, I believe that this is communion, and it seems to resonate with all kinds of people.

When our group grew to more than twenty, we formed two groups, so that we could continue to invite friends and keep the table open and inclusive. We have found mission to be natural in this context. But in my head I am still reticent to call this church and to relinquish my membership in a traditional church, and I am hesitant to say that the sharing of bread and wine on a Thursday night is a Eucharist.

The Lord's Supper: Formal rite or common meal?

Am I tied to Christendom notions of the Lord's Supper as a formal rite performed by set-aside individuals? Am I afraid of downgrading something so important and holy by collapsing it into the humble, sometimes hilarious, sometimes heartbreaking gathering around our table? Yet it seems to have so much more in common with my understanding of "Jesus, among friends gathered around the table, took bread . . ." and to be allied with the Shabbat meals I have had the privilege of sharing with Jewish friends. For contemporary people, starved of community and good home-cooked food, the coming together and acknowledging of the presence of Jesus among us seems to provide a new avenue through which to reconnect with the hospitable God who generously loves all creation.

Some may argue that this sort of practice is fine for house churches but impractical for larger church communities. Mirroring the hospitality of God is crucial for all church communities, particularly in these times when we are struggling to find authentic means of outreach. Most churches share meals occasionally, and such events can relatively easily be opportunities to do so "in remembrance of me." Whenever this happens, people hold fond memories of these events, and I would argue that it is worth the effort. To experience communion as a joyful communal thanksgiving, there needs to be a sense of community at the heart of it. People need to know and be learning to love one another. That happens best in shared activities such as eating together.

Our view of atonement can shape our experience of communion

The community also needs to know what it is thankful for. Another factor that seems to limit the missional dimension of communion is the preoccupation in many free church communities with stressing only one understanding of atonement. The heavy atmosphere of gloom and guilt that surrounds a labored exposition of the torture Jesus bore at the hands of God—"just for you"—does not energize a community into mission. Jonny Baker remembers his childhood experience of communion services as "very sombre. I got the impression that someone had died. Someone had, of course, but everyone seemed to have forgotten that he was resurrected and present in our midst."[9]

The depiction in Anselmian theories of atonement of Jesus as passive victim seems to engender a passive, slightly fearful piety, rather than an active engagement with the world. This view of Jesus sits uncomfortably with the one who continually defies convention, who proactively pushes boundaries and finds alternative approaches to promote shalom. Neither does it empower those who seek to follow Christ to take action in situations of injustice and abuse.

The Kreiders seem implicitly to endorse the Christus Victor approach to atonement as being both more true to early church thinking, and more tenable in a community committed to nonviolence and peacemaking. I believe that the community that gathers around a table to celebrate that Jesus has overcome the evil and brokenness of this world, through the power of love and sacrifice, is drawn into living that possibility for the here and now. As we share in the bread and wine, we become part of God's plan for the redemption of creation as we enflesh the life of Christ. What we do at the table then renews our passion to continue the work of Christ in the world, knowing that Jesus has overcome the powers of darkness, and that we are filled anew with his resurrection life.

Additionally, this understanding is more able to connect with post-Christendom pre-Christian minds who have no inbuilt conceptions of sin and guilt, but who do feel a radical disconnection at times between soul and body, and who live with a sense of powerlessness in the face of global and social issues.

The celebration of communion at its best not only sends Christians out renewed in their commitment to mission but is itself an evangelistic event in the best sense of the word. If we can find ways to tell God's story that can connect with contemporary thinking, and do so with good, interactive theatre and hospitality that connects with body and soul, then we might begin to understand why Jesus commanded us to repeat the events of the Last Supper.

[9] Jonny Baker, "Rhythm of the Masses," in *Mass Culture, Eucharist and Mission in a Post-modern World*, ed. Peter Ward (Oxford: Bible Reading Fellowship, 1999), 37.

I am so grateful for all the Kreiders have shaped in my life, for the many meals we have shared together, and for the way they live a joyful communal thanksgiving that gives life and integrity to all they teach and write.

⋮ John D. Rempel

I offer one response and propose one missing piece in our understanding of the Lord's Supper in relation to worship and mission. My response is to the Kreiders' four cautions to those who make the case for baptism as the pathway to the Eucharist. As to my proposal, a missing piece in many Protestant theologies of the Supper is an understanding of a sacrament as both a human and a divine act.

The cautions identify the underlying issue as the depth and breadth of the corporate life of the community. If that is not winsomely present, what are we welcoming people into when we invite them to break bread with us? Simply opening the Lord's Table to all who come, or simply reserving it for the baptized, does not adequately answer the question of whether a congregation is an embracing community. Those, like myself, who hold baptism to be the pathway to the Eucharist must cultivate a church in which baptism expresses a life of covenant with Christ and the church. They must foster relationships characterized by accountability and vulnerability that can be authentically expressed in rituals of hospitality.

And we must ask ourselves if we are embodying such community in true sacraments. This is the missing piece. Since the Enlightenment the practice of ritual has been regarded as a primitive expression of faith and belonging that has no role in a culture based on reason. Biblicistic Protestants have been surprisingly open to such analysis. They have often kept baptism and communion, the root symbols of the gospel, only because they are commanded in scripture. But in many Protestant settings they are "just" symbols—mere signs of what really matters, which is inward experience. For secular people, ritual expressions of inner states are regression from the light of reason into a magical state. Combinations of these mindsets shape many liberal and conservative arguments for open communion.

If, however, a sacrament is more than the sum of its rationally observable parts, someone's sincere quest for God is not the equivalent of the baptismal covenant. To call a symbol a sacrament is to believe that the Spirit actualizes God's saving work in baptism and Christ's real presence in the breaking of bread. If that is the case, an authentic human decision is only half of the equation. If baptism is the means by which God makes people part of Christ's body, it is more and other than the desire to belong; it is also the ritual in which God acts to make that belonging happen. Then there is not a one-to-one correlation between an individual's sincerity and her readiness to "eat and become the body of Christ" (Augustine).

God is sovereign and draws people to himself in ways beyond our reckoning. We must be ready to be interrupted by such acts of the Spirit. But Jesus gave us baptism and the Lord's Supper as the normal way of identifying God's work in individuals and congregations in the stylized and condensed way that constitutes a ritual act. In the realm of spirit there is a seamlessness between inner and outer, a co-witnessing by the Holy Spirit and the church that God has brought someone who turns to him for redemption. There is no separation between the outward and visible sign and the inward and invisible grace: the inward experience is completed in the outward act. This I learned from Pilgram Marpeck, sixteenth-century Anabaptist theologian, and Baptist New Testament scholar G. R. Beasley-Murray. This way of thinking has had a voice in churches that baptize on confession of faith over the centuries.

Especially in free churches, the question of communion without baptism is largely decided without regard for the nature of a sacrament. What is symbolized in initiation and communion is not simply a sincere human disposition but God's action. The missing piece is that baptism is not merely a depiction of an individual's intention toward God. If that were the case, baptism would be superfluous if the right intention were present. Baptism is equally the enactment of God's intention toward us; it is more than the sum of its rationally observable parts. We cannot be "re-membered" into

Christ and one another in the Eucharist if we have not first been "membered" into Christ and one another in baptism.

⦂ Laura Lehman Amstutz

What is the mood of a communion service? When I was a child growing up in a large Mennonite church twenty years ago, the overwhelming mood was solemn. This service communicated a seriousness and internal wrestling. I was a generation past public confession prior to communion, but that tradition still deeply informed the practice of communion. Communion was infrequent, maybe twice a year. The leaders still announced communion at least one Sunday ahead, so people could make themselves right with God and the community before partaking. And the congregation still practices "make-up communion" for those who missed worship on the Sunday when it was distributed.

On the other hand, my parents didn't take it quite so seriously. My father used to joke that on communion Sunday the elders met in the church kitchen to measure the bread cubes and make sure they were one inch by one inch square. And on several occasions my parents suggested that we should miss church because it was communion Sunday. I think their suggestion had to do not with being unprepared for communion but rather with the logistics of passing 500 thimbles of juice and bread cubes in a large sanctuary. As parents of an unruly teenager and an elementary school child, they probably did not find communion services easy to sit through.

Communion in this setting was neither the joyful, thankful communal act the Kreiders describe, nor the "narrative sacrament par excellence." It was shrouded in solemnity and became a ritual we needed to get through.

After seminary I began to attend The Table, an emerging congregation that focused on experimental worship. We began in 2007 with the intention of practicing communion every week. We had no history to contend with, and none of those ideas of "we always do it this way." This is not to say that practicing communion every week doesn't have its challenges. The how and when of communion can be difficult. We are constantly asking, "Where does communion fit into these texts and this message?" It does fit in every Sunday, because we shape the mood of communion to fit the theology of the scriptures for that Sunday.

Some Sundays, communion is the joyful affair the Kreiders describe. We have had "communion hoe-downs," when members of our congregation play fiddle and banjo as we partake. I once led a service in which communion was taken around tables in small groups and included not only bread and juice but peanut butter, honey, jam, and other toppings. Other Sundays, communion is a more solemn affair, taken in silence or after prayer of lament. I find each kind of service meaningful.

Does The Table take communion more or less seriously than the church of my childhood? A communion hoe-down looks very different from the solemn affair of my youth. There are aspects of my childhood congregation's practice that could get lost if The Table is not intentional about its practice. Where do we take seriously the call to confession? How do we remind ourselves of the responsibility to the community with which we partake? But I ask the congregation of my childhood, where is the joy in your celebration? And where do you explain the narrative surrounding a solemn and careful ritual? These are some of the questions the Kreiders' work prompts.

14

Multivoiced worship
Let all speak

Early Anabaptists understood worship and teaching in the congregation to be a multivoiced and dialogical activity. We see this perspective clearly in an untitled and unattributed tract of about forty pages, probably written in Switzerland in the 1530s. In tones both defensive and aggressive, the anonymous Anabaptist author answered a question commonly put to the radical reformers: Why don't you Anabaptists attend the (state) churches?

The Anabaptist's first reason for abandoning worship in the Reformed churches is that these churches do not observe "the Christian order as taught in the word of God in 1 Corinthians 14." According to that text, if something for edifying is revealed to believers during worship, Christian love compels "that they should and may speak of it"—after which they should again be silent. The author of the tract underlines Paul's emphasis on the desirability of the spiritual gifts, particularly the gift of prophecy, for the building up of the church.

In the Zurich state church, preachers kept a tight hold on their pulpits and allowed no informal contributions from the congregations. But the apostle Paul had commanded that no one should forbid speaking in tongues which serves to edify the congregation (1 Cor. 14:39). "How much less authority," our Anabaptist argues, "had anyone to forbid prophesying, teaching, interpreting or admonishing?"

The author passionately clinches his argument. "When someone comes to church and constantly hears only one person speaking and all the listeners are silent, neither speaking nor prophesying, who can . . . regard it to be a spiritual congregation? Or confess according to 1 Corinthians 14 that God is dwelling in them through his Holy Spirit with his gifts, impelling them one after the other to speak and prophesy?"

In the 1530s, as today, worship dominated by one voice blocks the Spirit's freedom to edify the church through the variety of gifts. In addition, the powerful single voice is beyond discernment and correction within the congregation. Our author concludes, "The church of Christ should together prove all things and hold fast to that which is good" (1 Thess. 5:21).[1]

....

⋮ Lloyd Pietersen

Anyone who has ever had the privilege of hearing Alan and Eleanor speak together knows that they embody the principle of multivoiced ministry. Their speaking resembles a dance, as each speaks with a distinctive voice, taking it in turns (sometimes even finishing the other's sentence!), and yet they speak as one. No one voice is predominant, and each is vital to the overall act of communication. To accomplish this is no small achievement—it comes from a lifetime together of mutual sharing, meditation, and deep listening.

Multivoiced worship and early Anabaptists

In the extract quoted above Eleanor draws on an Anabaptist tract, actually found within a major work directed against Anabaptists by Heinrich Bullinger (Ulrich Zwingli's successor at Zurich) and published in 1560. The tract was published in its entirety by Bullinger in order to refute Anabaptism.[2] As Eleanor rightly notes, it is highly significant that this tract puts the failure to engage in multivoiced worship, as Paul instructs in 1 Corinthians 14, as the first of its nine reasons for opposing attendance at the meetings of Reformed churches. Other objections include typical Anabaptist insistence on

---

[1] Reprinted from Eleanor Kreider, "A Vision of Multi-Voiced Worship: Involving the Whole People," *Anabaptism Today* 5 (February 1994): 13–14. Used by permission of the publisher.

[2] The text can be found in Shem Peachey and Paul Peachey, trans. and ed., "Answer of Some Who Are Called (Ana)Baptists Why They Do Not Attend the Churches: A Swiss Brethren Tract," *Mennonite Quarterly Review* 45, no. 1 (1971): 5–32.

behavior in keeping with the gospel, no coercion in matters of faith, the eschewal of violence, and the critique of infant baptism.

But the lack of multivoiced worship stands first! The writer recognized that the Protestant Reformers had not altered centuries of ecclesial tradition. "In keeping with a tradition over a thousand years old, preachers kept a tight hold on their pulpits and allowed no informal contributions from the congregations."[3] Furthermore, the writer astutely judges the lack of multivoiced worship in Reformed congregations to demonstrate a profound dearth of congregational spirituality. "When someone comes to church and constantly hears only one person speaking, and all the listeners are silent, neither speaking nor prophesying, who can or will regard or confess the same to be a spiritual congregation, or confess according to 1 Cor. 14 that God is dwelling and operating in them through his Holy Spirit with his gifts?"[4]

As I reread Eleanor's article in conjunction with the sixteenth-century Anabaptist tract, I was reminded of what powerfully attracted me to what became known as the "house church" or "new church" movement in its early days. Recognizing the deficiencies of the model in which a single priest, vicar, or pastor presides over the whole service, and the perceived dry formalism of the liturgy in traditional denominations, house churches emphasized the contribution of every member to the ongoing life of the community and championed spontaneity in worship. If the charismatic movement generally emphasized the gifts of the Spirit of 1 Corinthians 12:4–11, the house church movement built on this by focusing on the contribution of every member in a community characterized by love (1 Cor. 12:12–14:40). Indeed, I still remember a remarkable address to a packed audience of house church members from across Britain in the mid-1970s, in which, based on 1 Corinthians 14:26, the congregation was exhorted to put into practice "every-member ministry."

---

[3] Kreider, "A Vision of Multi-Voiced Worship," 14.

[4] Peachey and Peachey, trans. and ed., "Answer," 11.

Every-member ministry in the house church movement

In the early days, when these congregations were small and generally literally met in houses, meetings were genuinely multivoiced,
every contribution was valued, and no distinction was made on the
basis of gender. In those days the predominant metaphors for the
church that resonated with us were, ecclesiologically, the church as
the *body of Christ* (every-member "body ministry") and, eschatologi-
cally, the church as the *bride of Christ* (preparing for the return of
the bridegroom). First Corinthians 12–14, Ephesians 5:25–33, and
Revelation 19:6–9 were thus key texts.

However, over time (to simplify greatly) two significant things
happened.[5] First, the movement was successful and experienced
spectacular growth, resulting in much larger congregations. In
this context the sheer size of the congregation militated against
genuinely multivoiced worship, and although house churches never
forgot their roots, so that church services were never single-voiced,
nevertheless the norm became few voices, with a renewed emphasis
on the preacher on the one hand and the role of the worship group
on the other. As Eleanor rightly states:

> The sixteenth-century Anabaptist critique of single-voice
> worship raises questions of how Christians today can be most
> faithful to a New Testament model of corporate life. Congrega-
> tional worship dominated "from the front" is to be found in . . .
> churches led by a single pastor and in those led by music/wor-
> ship groups. Both types must address the question of balancing
> responsibilities of designated leadership with the necessities of
> developing the gifts of all the members.[6]

Eleanor is also critical of "the assumption that successful churches
will be large ones. There is nothing more 'Constantinian' in the

---

[5] For more detailed analysis see L. K. Pietersen, "Ecstatic Phenomena for an
Ecstatic Culture?" in *The Mark of the Spirit? A Charismatic Critique of the "Blessing"
Phenomenon*, ed. L. K. Pietersen (Carlisle, Cumbria, England: Paternoster Press,
1998), 7–32.

[6] Kreider, "A Vision of Multi-Voiced Worship," 15.

life of our churches," she writes, "than the assumption that big is beautiful."[7]

Second, the eschatological emphasis slowly began to predominate, but now with a subtle twist. Instead of the early emphasis on the "bride making herself ready" (Rev. 19:7), the emphasis increasingly shifted to the role of "Ephesians 4 ministries" in bringing the church to maturity (Eph. 4:11–16). Now, everyone was encouraged "to find their ministry," with "ministry" largely defined in Ephesians 4:11 terms. This quickly became an emphasis on "*first* apostles, *second* prophets, *third* teachers" (1 Cor. 12:28) so that every-member ministry was transformed into a male-dominated hierarchy. The spirit of Constantine had not been sufficiently exorcised! Although things have changed significantly since, not least in the role now accorded to women, nevertheless the movement in my view has strayed far from its household roots and in doing so has tragically lost much of its multivoiced character.

The interplay between "crowd" and "little flock" in Luke's Gospel

I, too, echo Eleanor's concerns about large churches, because big congregations all too often display a crowd mentality. In this connection I have been struck again by the interplay between Jesus, the crowd, and the disciples in Luke 12. The chapter begins with a crowd in the thousands (12:1), and this grouping is deliberately contrasted with the group of disciples, whom Jesus addresses as a "little flock" (12:32). On several occasions in this extraordinary chapter, the narrative shifts focus between the crowd and the disciples in such a way as to challenge readers to consider whether they are part of the crowd or are among Jesus' disciples.

The two, at least according to Luke 12, are mutually exclusive. The first mention of crowds in Luke occurs in 3:7, where John the Baptist refers to them as a "brood of vipers." As the narrative moves forward, the reader observes ambivalence about the crowds. In 4:42 the crowds find Jesus in a deserted place and try to keep hold of him. Although Jesus escapes, he continues to teach the crowds and

[7] Ibid., 17.

to heal them. Yet already in 5:15–16 we see the tension between the demands of the crowds and Jesus' own strategy of withdrawal to the desert. In 6:17–19 we get a vivid picture of the crowds pressing in on Jesus to touch him. The spectacle of healing draws the masses, and in 9:11 we find Jesus welcoming the crowd. However, immediately after this incident Jesus begins to draw a distinction between the crowds and the disciples. In 9:18–20 he asks the disciples who the crowds think he is, and then he asks who *they* think he is. In 11:14–16 we discover that crowds are not homogeneous. They are amazed at his healing, but some accuse him of being in league with Beelzebul, while others keep demanding a sign in order to test him.

In 11:29, as the crowds increase, Jesus describes the current generation as evil and specifically links this observation to their request for a sign, as already remarked on in 11:16. Now in 12:1 the crowd numbers in the thousands, and the Gospel writer highlights the danger of such a large gathering: "they trampled on one another." But in this context Jesus does not address the crowd; he turns specifically to his disciples (12:1b). Twelve verses later, in response to a question from the crowd, Jesus addresses them in 12:13–21, and then it is back once again to the disciples in 12:22–40. This interplay between the crowd and the disciples is made more explicit in 12:41 when Peter asks Jesus whether he is addressing the preceding parable just to his disciples or to everyone. Whomever 12:42–53 is addressed to, Jesus specifically returns to the crowds in 12:54.

Will you be a disciple or one of the crowd?

The explicit challenge to the reader is this: will you become a disciple or be part of the crowd? To be a disciple is to be a member of the "little flock" (12:32), rather than one of the thousands. The crowd is concerned with possessions (12:13), and Jesus accuses them of not understanding the times and of not being able to judge what is right (12:54–57). He urges disciples to beware the hypocrisy of the Pharisees (12:1) and then addresses the crowd as hypocrites (12:56). Disciples will be persecuted, and are to sell their possessions and give themselves to serving the Lord. While the crowd is concerned for material inheritance, Jesus promises the kingdom as his disciples' inheritance.

Instead of allowing the huge numbers in the crowd to give him affirmation, Jesus deliberately turns first to his small band of disciples and speaks not of adulation but of persecution. In a later incident, when once again Luke refers to "large crowds," Jesus speaks of the costs of discipleship and challenges the crowds to carry the cross—a clear reference to living a lifestyle completely at odds with the dominant system.

Jesus' reference to the disciples as a flock echoes texts such as Isaiah 40:11, Jeremiah 31:10, and Ezekiel 34:12, but in none of those texts is "flock" qualified by "little." Furthermore, one verse in this section (12:32) has no parallel in Matthew; it is uniquely Lukan. It is impossible for multiple voices to be heard in a crowd. I am increasingly convinced that the "little flock" is the appropriate context for multivoiced worship, mutual accountability, and appropriate discipleship.

Multivoiced worship fosters congregational discernment

Finally, another significant aspect of multivoiced worship that both Eleanor and the Anabaptist tract draw attention to concerns its significance in promoting congregational discernment. When every member is encouraged not only to contribute but to exercise discernment both in learning when to be silent and in weighing the contributions of others (1 Cor. 14:29–30), then real congregational maturity can be fostered. A congregation that learns to question together, not in a critical spirit but in an environment of genuine love and mutual affection, will know that what emerges from such testing will be something to hold fast to (1 Thess. 5:21). An examination of the semantic field of discernment in the New Testament warrants careful study, but that subject takes us beyond the purpose of this particular essay. Suffice it to say that the New Testament abounds in "discernment" words, including *anakrinō* ("to examine closely"),[8] *diakrinō* ("to give judgment"),[9] *diakri-*

---

[8] For example, Acts 17:11 and 1 Cor. 2:14–15; 14:24.

[9] For example, 1 Cor. 6:5; 11:29; and 14:29.

sis ("differentiation"),[10] *dokimazō* ("to put to the test"),[11] and others. Because the earliest church was born in the context of "many gods and many lords" (1 Cor. 8:5) in the Greco-Roman world competing for its attention, congregational discernment was crucial. This need for wise discernment is just as vital today, when in so many circles there is pressure to respond to the latest fad and where all too often "the powerful single voice is beyond discernment and correction within the congregation."

I am so grateful to God for Alan and Eleanor. Neither of them can ever be described as "one of the crowd." Their friendship means much to my wife, Sheila, and me, and they have always modeled careful listening and critical discernment.

⁞ Tony Richie

Providentially, my personal introduction to the Kreiders involved a context of multivoiced worship. In an ecumenical dialogue between Mennonite Church USA and the Church of God (with International Offices in Cleveland, Tennessee) at Reba Place Church in Evanston, Illinois (2006), participants first shared table fellowship and then moved into the sanctuary for corporate worship. At dinner, the Lord blessed me to be seated next to Alan. We had the most wonderful time together! Christ's grace so beautifully ministered to me through this godly brother. After dinner, our worship included singing and dancing as well as prayer and testimony. Every person shared a word of personal testimony. Every voice was lifted distinctively in hopeful faith and love. I vividly remember a profound sense of the Holy Spirit's presence. God was glorified in our midst, and we were edified in God's presence.

I am a third-generation Pentecostal Christian by my family faith heritage. Ingrained in me is an idea that when the Spirit of Pentecost is present in power, then worship can encompass and

---

[10] For example, 1 Cor. 12:10; Heb. 5:14.

[11] For example, Rom. 12:2; 1 Cor. 11:28; 2 Cor. 8:8, 22; 13:5; Gal. 6:4; Eph. 5:10; Phil. 1:10; 1 Thess. 5:21; and 1 Tim. 3:10.

transcend gender, age, socioeconomic status, and other identities (see Acts 2:17–18). Worship is worthy of everyone's involvement. Understandably, therefore, I find Eleanor Kreider's writing and Lloyd Pietersen's reflections on this matter intriguing and challenging. I am intrigued, because as Anabaptists and Pentecostals, each distinctive in our own way, we nonetheless share a commitment to worship that is not impoverished in a monophonic solo but enriched by a polyphonic choir of full-orbed voices ascending in worship to God through our common Savior and Lord. Of course, I heartily applaud early Anabaptist appreciation for spiritual gifts in 1 Corinthians 14 as indicative and illustrative of this reality.

I am challenged, because I fear that contemporary Christians could all too easily lose or let slip the sound of diversity-in-unity in worship. A constant temptation, it seems to me, is to stifle voices that seem dissonant at first hearing but in reality can be deeply resonant if we listen together closely. Thus, I find Pietersen's insistence on discernment most apropos. Diversity does not equal anarchy, just as uniformity by no means guarantees unity. *Unity is complexity in solidarity!* I think Pentecostals and Anabaptists, and perhaps many other Christians, need to hear well Eleanor Kreider's voice on this matter of multivoiced worship.

I have sometimes wondered whether ecumenism, in an effort to achieve visible, or audible, unity—to which I am committed—can tend to blend or blur various voices. Perhaps Radical Reformation heirs are more comfortable with an element of cacophony—at least so long as there is an underlying cadence uniting us in Christ through the fellowship of the Spirit (Phil. 2:1) and sweet simplicity of the gospel (2 Cor. 11:3). So then, let us *all* speak—and worship!—in various tongues while allowing the Holy Spirit the right to interpret (Acts 2:4). With the Kreiders, I believe that healthy Christian living makes ample room for multiple voices in the faith of Christ.

⋮ Glen Marshall

I am convinced. Breaking up liturgical monopoly has to be the way to go. But let's not kid ourselves. To welcome genuine multivocal worship is to invite discord.

Even if we are successful in our attempts to get more people to pipe up, we will not likely recapture Lloyd Pietersen's fond memory of the Kreiders' synchronized liturgical duets where "each speaks with a distinctive voice . . . and yet they speak as one." Certainly Jesus' little flock didn't always bleat along to the same tune. But it seems to me that this is no bad thing.

Isn't it true that the fuller understanding of discipleship—toward which Jesus' band of followers eventually stumbled—often emerged from the encounter of *divergent* voices? Staying with Luke as our guide, learning about greatness at the back end of chapter nine is one example.

Multivocal worship, as the Corinthians knew all too well, is not always *comfortable* worship. I, myself, have been on the receiving end of a number of hair-raising heckles while I was preaching. The most memorable of these were rather robust and expressed in, shall we say, unecclesiastical language! Surely we don't want to risk that kind of thing. Well, I'm not convinced.

I've been intrigued for a while now by Kathryn Tanner's description of the church as "a community of argument concerning the meaning of true discipleship."[12] While not wanting to encourage liturgical slanging matches, I do like the way the word *argument* suggests heartfelt engagement from a variety of perspectives about something that matters to all concerned. Rather *this* than bored chitchat about inconsequential fripperies.

I also like the challenge that Tanner's phrase presents to that other Constantinian construct—an overbearing, monolithic conception of orthodoxy. What matters about being church is not that we manage to get all our iotas lined up neatly, but that together we

---

[12] See Kathryn Tanner, *Theories of Culture: A New Agenda for Theology,* Guides to Theological Inquiry (Minneapolis: Augsburg Fortress, 1997), 156.

work at thrashing out what it means for us right here, right now, to follow Christ.

If that is to happen, then the more voices in worship the better. Please, God, we don't need more of the same. Let's have more women's voices, more young people, more African voices, more Asian, more people with disabilities, more elderly voices—in short, more of all sorts of voices, more difference. It's the only way we will ever get to hear all the rich overtones in the voice of Christ.

I guess I'm asking for a dose of realism. If we do manage to embrace a wider range of voices when we worship, we can also bid farewell to any guarantee of harmony. There is bound to be dissonance, but that is good. Dissonance is musical spice, the antidote to saccharine slush. Too much harmony is not good for us.

So, down with liturgical monotony! Raise your voices for polyphony! Bring on the dissonance! Open our ears, Lord. We want to hear Jesus.

15

Worship and mission
Breathe in and out

It is because of the character and purpose of God that worship and mission are intertwined. Neither worship nor mission can take precedence over the other. Neither has the right to specialize itself and to declare that it can exist without symbiotic relationship with the other.

The Christendom years show us that worship—as an activity that humans can control—tends to take precedence over mission. In Christendom, worship was the province of the religious professionals, the clergy. Within the past century this has changed. According to John Witvliet, "The growth of lay worship leaders has arguably been one of the most sweeping liturgical changes in the past century."[1] This change has brought renewed life to many in the church, and it will reach its potential when the worship led by the lay worship leaders equips the worshiping communities with a vision of the mission of God and empowers and emboldens them to take part in it.

If the church is to have a future in post-Christendom, there must be renewed emphasis on mission, which is something that only God can control. There must be as many workshops and training weekends that alert people to God's mission and equip them to participate in it as there are on worship. Mission must join worship at the heart of the church's life, for in post-Christendom—after the supports of a sympathetic state and public have disappeared— "non-missional churches will not survive."[2]

---

[1] John Witvliet, *Worship Seeking Understanding* (Grand Rapids, MI: Baker, 2003), 271.

[2] Stuart Murray, *Church after Christendom* (Milton Keynes, Buckinghamshire, England: Paternoster, 2004), 146.

*But how satisfying, how sanctifying it is when Christians see worship
and mission not dualistically, not in competition, but as the integrated
action of a body that is made whole. We can view it as a gathering and
sending—for we cannot spend all of our time in the Christian assembly,
and we cannot survive in our work if we do not gather to worship God.
However, we find it more helpful to view the Christian life—with the
worship and mission that are integral to it—as a matter of breathing.
"The Church's existence is a continual alternation between two phases.
Like systole and exhalation in the process of breathing, assembly and
mission succeed each other in the life of the Church. Discipleship would
be stunted unless it included both the centripetal phase of worship and the
centrifugal phase of mission."[3]*

So wrote the late Cardinal Avery Dulles in his classic Models of the
Church. *He understands the deep synergy that, by God's design, there
is between worship and mission. His observation negates assertions that
worship is more important than mission (as it was in Christendom), or
that mission is more important than worship (as it is in the view of some
activists). Is inhaling more important than exhaling? Or exhaling than
inhaling? There is instead a deep wholeness to which God calls us. God
calls individual Christians, churches of all sorts, theological colleges and
seminaries, bishops, pastors, and church bureaucrats to seek this wholeness
vigilantly, critically, and above all hopefully. For through it all the mission of God is coursing. The reconciliation of people to God, of people to
the estranged other, of people to the created order that we pillage—this
vision is nurtured in worship services and embodied in lives of worshipful
service.*

*It is God whose work brings cosmic reconciliation. It is Jesus Christ
through whom God has definitively reconciled the world to God. It is the
Holy Spirit who continues to nurture, nudge, and blaze forth to enable
the impossible to happen. And we? We are God's children, God's servants,
who ascribe worth to God by breathing in—worshiping the Lord with*

---

[3] Avery Dulles, *Models of the Church*, 2nd ed. (New York: Doubleday, 1987), 220.

gladness—and by breathing out—collaborating with God as God continues the story and brings the peaceable kingdom.[‡]

....

⫶ Janet Plenert

The week was so heavy. The USA had declared war and entered Iraq. On Saturday we joined a peace march, even though it felt like such a small act. We were tempted by hopelessness. But Sunday was coming, and I looked forward to worshiping, lamenting, praying with others about what appeared to be a step away from peace in the world. Sunday came. The pre-planned, orchestrated worship service was executed seamlessly and efficiently. But the newly declared war was never mentioned. I felt betrayed and empty. As I left the service, I wondered if the church was actually as irrelevant and ineffectual as it seemed.

At a worship service in Brazil, a semi-incoherent, out-of-place voice disrupted the service. It came from a disheveled man I didn't know. He walked in, mumbling, greeting people in a way that made sense only to him. His unstable gait confirmed his inebriated state. The worship leaders paused as they publicly welcomed him, and others made space for him to sit. The people near him focused their attention on him, checking on how he was, what his name was. It was clear that sitting in the service wasn't what he needed. Several lay leaders invited him to talk and pray, and a small group helped him walk safely into an area at the back and began to listen to him and pray with him. Worship leaders spontaneously added a prayer time to the worship service, praying for this man. It seemed natural to incorporate this "interruption" by altering the flow of the service, and to minister to the needs of a lonely, drunken person.

[‡] Reprinted from *Worship and Mission after Christendom*, by Alan and Eleanor Kreider. Copyright © 2011 by Herald Press, Scottdale PA 15683. Used by permission.

If today's church fails to correct the legacy of Christendom, it will die

We worship the true, creating God of love with all of our lives, ascribing worth to this God, our Lord (Rom. 12:1–2; Matt. 6:24). And we participate in God's mission of shalom-building, kingdom-coming, reconciling and gathering up all things—all things in heaven and all things on earth (Col. 1:20). Worship and mission belong together, as Alan and Eleanor Kreider have carefully modeled and taught, and have inspired the church throughout their ministry.

We are victims of the success of Christendom. Both the church and the state declared that everyone within a given political territory was also Christian and part of the church. Christian mission within that geographical territory was not needed any more. Mission lost its place as an integral part of the life and vocation of the body of Christ. The life of the church, then, focused on worship, as defined and executed by the clergy. Worship and mission were separated from each other. We continue to live with the legacy of this once-churched, dichotomized world. This means that the church is too often seen as a sluggish institution, defending its tradition and irrelevant for the transformation of the world. Our post-Christendom church must challenge and change this legacy, or it will die.

The worship of God's children should send them into God's mission

We long for a Holy Spirit transformed, reconciled, and reshaped world in which every tribe and nation bows before the Lord and all things on earth are restored. And we long for a church that is an agent of radical change and hope for the world.

The worship of God's children should acknowledge, be shaped by, create understanding of, and send us into the mission of God. Whether our context is a newly declared war, or a systemic, deeply rooted cultural issue that needs Christ's liberating and healing touch, we need worship to empower and sustain us as we participate in God's mission around us. We must not continue to plan worship services with the Christendom assumption that worship is discon-

nected from mission. The God we love and serve has come to reconcile and make right the world we have messed up. Our worship
must reflect this reality and equip us for participation with God in
making things right.

We must find ways to more fully ascribe glory to our God, who
wants not only to be in right relationship with individuals but also
to address global injustice, child poverty, stewardship of the earth,
political regimes, relationships between First Nations peoples and
those who came to live on their land, and relationships with our
enemies. This agenda for worship goes beyond a desire to be seeker
sensitive, and it assumes that not only believers steeped in church
culture will attend.

Engagement in God's mission should lead us back to worship

Similarly, our mission efforts must lead us into worship. Too often
we spin ministries off into professionalized specialties and detach
them from their source and rightful place. Thus, for example, peace
becomes a task relegated to activists rather than a lived vocation
of the church; creation care is assigned to nonprofit organizations;
conflict resolution is given to professionals, including the armed
forces; and evangelism is the role of missionaries who have crossed
an ocean to do it. When such tasks are detached from the church or
are peripheral to it, the church is relegated to being a limited and
somewhat impotent body whose purpose is still the Christendom
purpose of providing corporate worship opportunities, disconnected from mission, for believers.

Yet the creating God of life has a much bigger purpose: to reconcile to God all things, whether on earth or in heaven, by making peace through the blood of Christ (Eph. 1:10; 2:11–14). This
unimaginably large purpose is God's mission, which God has chosen to enact through God's keynote creation: the body of Christ,
which is the church. The apostle Paul indicates that the mystery of
the good news has been revealed to us so that "through the church"
(Eph. 3:10) all things can be made as God intends. The gifts we
have been given are not for the sake of our professional specialty

but for the building up of the body (Eph. 4:12), so that we will come to full measure in Christ, *so that through the church* we might work with God in fulfilling God's mission. Therefore our mission efforts, even enacted as ministry specializations, must necessarily point us back to God, back to God's purposes, and back to the very act of ascribing worth to God in worship. We must reintegrate worship and mission as two parts of an inseparable vocation—that of being the body of Christ.

Worship and mission *can* go hand in hand, as parts of a great whole

In Congo millions of people live in bondage to fear. Whether Christian or not, they believe in, are affected by, and fear evil spirits manifested through many forms of witchcraft. Early missionaries did not understand this fear. They were confident that Jesus had won the victory over death and over evil, and they planted churches that often did not adequately acknowledge or address the fear of evil spirits. The fear did not simply go away when people became Christians. Their worship in church ignored this critical aspect of the liberating, restoring mission of God in their context. The music used in services, for instance, was translated from other cultural sources, and it did not adequately address the mission God has in liberating, healing, restoring, and reconciling these people in their context.

But worship and mission can go hand in hand, as parts of a greater whole. Situated across the Pearl River Delta from Hong Kong is the former Portuguese colony of Macau. This city-state has overtaken Las Vegas as the gambling capital of the world. Beginning a church in this challenging context is a painstaking endeavor. Worship must radiate rooted hope and tangible peace, and the church must model faithfulness, focus, satisfaction derived from the love of God alone. It must point to the fact that relationships can be both transformed and transformative. The small Mennonite church in Macau is using a wonderful litany created by Eleanor Kreider. It is a call to live our worship experience with God in practical and tangible ways throughout our daily lives. The leader poses questions, and the people respond.

> *Whom do we love?*
> We love the Lord our God.
> *How do we love God?*
> With all our hearts, with all our minds, with all our souls, and with all our strength.

> *Whom do we love?*
> We love our neighbors.
> *How do we love our neighbors?*
> As we love ourselves.

> *Whom do we love?*
> We love our enemies.
> *How do we love our enemies?*
> We pray for them and we bless them.

In this context, where Christians are a tiny minority and love of money shapes the culture, this simple yet profound, biblically based liturgy reminds God's people of God's very character and purpose of reconciling all things to God. It roots them for the coming week and gives strength to live faithfully. We love God with our whole lives, our beings, our hearts, our thoughts, our vocations, our time, our attitudes. Love is also for those we encounter in our jobs, in our families, in our apartment complexes; it is for those who do not believe or understand that we can believe. Love is equally for our enemies—for those who oppress us, for those who disown us for our faith, for the parents who wanted their only child to be a son and were given a daughter, for those whose attention we crave and who don't have time for us in a busy gambling world. This litany is a pedagogical tool that sends the church from its worship time into ordinary lives to live as Christ did, transforming and reconciling and setting right everything in heaven and on earth.

Together, in balanced rhythm, worship and mission enable life

I long for worship to recapture its proper place among God's people as something that flows out of our souls and is affected by our activities throughout the week. I long for God's mission, carried out through the church, to be understood as our critical and world-transforming vocation for our everyday lives. It is this vocation that pulls us back into worship. I long for our worship songs to reflect the holistic, all-encompassing shalom that flows from God's heart. I long for them to address the challenges of God's mission in our contexts. I long for everyday, messy stories of God's transformative love experienced in the lives of everyday people to be integrated into weekly worship services. I long for worship that gives expression to both the brokenness and the joy of our world and invites us to mold our lives to be more Christ-like.

I long for the language we use to be inclusive, sensitive, and accessible for those who are marginalized or who are new to the faith. I long for us to take seriously the advice of our sisters and brothers in other parts of the world, when they tell us that we have become so efficient in planning our congregational activities that there is no room for the Holy Spirit to move, invade, and surprise us. I long for our worship services to reveal the multifaceted, grand, almost unimaginable purposes of God. I long for our specialized efforts to be rooted in the church, sent out from the church, and lead back to the church.

As important as it is, worship by itself should not be the center around which all other activities of God's people are organized. The Kreiders have helpfully illustrated and demonstrated that worship and mission, in their broadest, most magnificent, holistic, and undichotomized forms, should be like breathing in and breathing out—each begging for the other, each preparing the way and clearing the path for the other, each providing the substance the other needs in order to exist. On its own and without the other, each causes the organism to choke and ultimately die. But together, in balanced rhythm, worship and mission enable life.

May God grant grace and courage to the church, that we might remember and enable God's grand mission in worship. And may our participation in God's mission compel us with love into worship. And may we find our resting place in the God of mission who is both the subject and the object of our worship.

⠇ Marty Troyer

"I don't want to be here," I shouted recently to a crowd of workers seeking livable compensation as janitors in Houston, Texas. "I'd rather be with family, or reading a nice book. So why am I here? I'm here because God is working to create a world where everyone is fed, where people receive a living wage, and where you're not judged by the color of your skin or excluded because you're a recent immigrant. The world God is working to create is filled with justice, right relationships, and love. But that is not our world! Our world is full of greed, hatred, exclusion. Our world needs more people like you, people willing to do what Jesus did, so we can one day say that God's kingdom has come on earth like it is in heaven. And because of that, there is no place I'd rather be!"

When I first met Alan and Eleanor Kreider several years ago, I was not this bold. Burned out from being misplaced in a ministry position, doubting my faith, and stripped of confidence in self and call, I entered seminary assuming God had forgotten me and hoping the church soon would. I sought the "good life," free of sacrifice and concern for anyone but family, and with little energy for a mission I doubted even existed. Attending Sunday worship was my only real faith practice. But it was here, worshiping in gathered community, that I was formed to love the mission of God.

Worship and its practices gave me a beautiful view of the world as God is working for it to be—filled with love, joy, justice, and peace on earth as it is in heaven. This is a world where lambs sleep beside lions, weapons are transformed into tools because they are no longer needed, all people know their belovedness as part of meaningful community, and God is in control. How did worship captivate me for Christ's kingdom? Through open mic sharing time

I experienced genuine community and acceptance; receiving offerings gave me a glimpse of people responding to brokenness in the world; singing reminded me of the presence of God; teachings channeled my best energies; communion challenged me to enter Jesus' story as participant with Christ in breaking and pouring myself out for the world; and benedictions were weekly invitations.

Alan and Eleanor have an amazing ability to discern when people's lives, the feel of a filled room, or the world itself is pregnant with Spirit, and to connect people with the mission of God. They've done this repeatedly for me. They helped me see that worship is genuine contact with myself, the world, God, and God's mission. Ultimately, it was nothing more or less than worship that formed me to partner with God for God's kingdom to come on earth as it is in heaven. Why do I do what I do? Because in worshiping, I fell in love with the mission of God. May it be so for us all!

Sally Schreiner Youngquist

I first recall meeting the Kreiders on a visit to their Oxford home in 1997. I could see how their holistic weaving together of prayer, peace, mission, service, and contextual analysis had helped make Anabaptism attractive to disciples seeking to reclaim the vitality of Christianity in the post-Christian West.

My own Chicago context has stretched me to take prayer and worship into the streets to address the powers of violence in our neighborhood. As an urban church-planting team, our first act of public worship came in response to a shooting of one student by another outside the local high school. The following Sunday we carried a large wooden cross to the site and prayed prayers for healing of the injured parties and for the return of peace to the neighborhood. A few neighbors in this multicultural community joined us, noticing the cross and hearing the prayers. Police surveyed us from patrol cars, alert to the possibility of gang reprisals.

Occasional shootings followed over the years, summoning us to claim and reclaim the neighborhood as Christ's rightful domain. We often walked the streets in small groupings to pray at neighborhood trouble spots. A fatal shooting on the corner of Pratt and Ashland motivated our youth to begin a weekly Sunday night prayer vigil there for several years. This in turn led to the purchase of the storefront at this location as the meetinghouse for Living Water Community Church. The congregation and many visiting work groups put in hours of sweat equity to transform the building into a house of worship. Work and worship went hand in hand as youth inscribed scripture verses under the drywall, disabled and homeless folk joined our volunteer workforce, and prayer services and parties were hosted at the construction site. "Called to the corner to participate in Christ's work of reconciliation in our church, neighborhood, and world" became our church mission statement.

The building gave us a street level location from which to offer worship, after-school programs, vacation Bible schools, English classes, and community meeting space. We collaborated with CeaseFire, a city-wide coalition of churches, social service agencies, and street workers dedicated to eliminating gun violence as a leading cause of death for young people. After each local shooting, we were invited to march and lead prayers at the site of violence. Often the only clergy present, I was asked to lead the prayers. I tried to be sensitive to the interfaith nature of our neighborhood, creating a litany inviting simple participation from whoever would join us. Carrying a small jug of water, I would sprinkle the ground with water as an act of cleansing.

As Mennonite peacemakers, we have sometimes been criticized by law-and-order types as being "soft on crime." We try to offer prayer evenhandedly for all affected parties, believing God cares equally for all. I have come to believe that, no matter how few or many are gathered for such a vigil, we are called to witness to the principalities and powers that this is God's turf, not theirs (Eph. 3:10). Being "called to the corner" has taught us to "breathe in and breathe out" in increasingly risky, inclusive ways to claim the neighborhood as our parish.

Bibliography of published writings of Alan and Eleanor Kreider

1963

Kreider, Alan. "Lancaster County Politics, 1799–1810." *Journal of the Lancaster County Historical Society* 67 (1963): 1–22, 33–43.

1969

Kreider, Alan. "To Make a Revolution." *Christian Graduate* 23 (1969), 2–9.

———, and Kenneth A. Lockridge. "The Evolution of Massachusetts Town Government, 1640–1740." *William and Mary Quarterly*, 3rd ser., 23 (1969): 549–74.

Reprinted in *Colonial America: Essays in Politics and Social Development*, edited by Stanley N. Katz (Boston: Little Brown and Co., 1971); and in *Perspectives of the American Experience* I, edited by Marvin Meyers and J. R. Pole (Glenview, IL: Scott, Foresman and Co., 1971), 75–88.

1972

Kreider, Alan. "The Way of Christ." In *Is Revolution Change?* edited by Brian Griffiths, 46–69. London: Inter-Varsity Press, 1972.

Reprint, in expanded form, of "To Make a Revolution (1969).

1974

Kreider, Alan. "Why Revolution?" *Spectrum* 6, no. 3 (May 1974), 4–7.

1975

Kreider, Alan. "Assassination, a Superficial Technique." *Viewpoint* (Inter-School Christian Fellowship) 30 (1975), 12–14.

————. "The Christian and the State in Revolutionary Times: The Anabaptists." In *The Christian and the State in Revolutionary Times: Being Papers Read at the 1975 Conference*, edited by Graham Harrison, 28–44. Huntingdon, Cambridgeshire, England: Westminster Conference, 1975.

————. "Christianity and Social Responsibility." *Reformation Today* 26 (July-August 1975): 31–36.

————. "An English Episcopal Draft Article against the Anabaptists, 1536." *Mennonite Quarterly Review* 49 (1975): 38–42.

————. "The Origins of Revolution (Some Insights from the Social Sciences)." *Spectrum* 7, no. 2 (January 1975), 4–7.

————. "The Origins of Revolution." *Spectrum* 8, no. 1 (September 1975), 4–6, 34–35.

The editors of *Spectrum* by mistake repeated the title of the January 1975 article; the September 1975 article was to have been entitled "The Two Faces of Revolution."

————. "The U.S. Bicentennial." *Gospel Herald* 21 (October 1975), 1–3.

Reprinted in *The Mennonite*, October 28, 1975; and *Mennonite Reporter*, November 10, 1975.

1976

Kreider, Alan. "Revolution—The Alternatives." *Spectrum* 8, no. 3 (1976), 4–6, 30–32, 41.

1977

Kreider, Alan. "John Foxe." In *The History of Christianity: A Lion Handbook*, edited by Tim Dowley, 24. Berkhamsted, Hertfordshire, England: Lion Publishing, 1977.

The History of Christianity: A Lion Handbook was published in the US as *The Eerdmans Handbook of Church History* (Grand Rapids, MI: Eerdmans, 1977).

————, and John H. Yoder. "The Anabaptists." In *The History of Christianity: A Lion Handbook*, edited by Tim Dowley, 401–5. Berkhamsted, Hertfordshire, England: Lion Publishing, 1977.

The History of Christianity: A Lion Handbook was published in the US as *The Eerdmans Handbook of Church History* (Grand Rapids, MI: Eerdmans, 1977).

————, and John H. Yoder. "Christians and War." In *The History of Christianity: A Lion Handbook*, edited by Tim Dowley, 51–54. Berkhamsted, Hertfordshire, England: Lion Publishing, 1977.

The History of Christianity: A Lion Handbook was published in the US as *The Eerdmans Handbook of Church History* (Grand Rapids, MI: Eerdmans, 1977).

1979

Kreider, Alan. *English Chantries: The Road to Dissolution.* Harvard Historical Studies 97. Cambridge, MA: Harvard University Press, 1979.

Received Honorable Mention, the John Ben Snow Prize of the North American Conference on British Studies, 1982.

1980

Hornus, Jean-Michel. *It Is Not Lawful for Me to Fight: Early Christian Attitudes toward War, Violence, and the State,* rev. ed. Translated by Alan Kreider and Oliver Coburn. Scottdale, PA: Herald Press, 1980.

Kreider, Alan. "Biblical Perspectives on War." *Third Way,* November 1980, 13–14.

————. "Turnabout for Evangelical Leaders." *Towards Renewal,* Summer 1980, 14–15.

————. *War to End All Wars.* Nottingham, Nottinghamshire: Shaftesbury Project, 1980.

Text and annotations for slide-tape presentation.

1981

Kreider, Alan. "The Pacifism of the Early Church: An Ecumenical Heritage." *Sojourners*, January 1981, 28–29.

Reprinted in many periodicals, and in *A Matter of Faith: A Study Guide for Churches on the Nuclear Arms Race* (Washington, DC: Sojourners Fellowship, 1981), 44–45; in *Waging Peace: A Handbook for the Struggle to Abolish Nuclear Weapons*, edited by Jim Wallis (San Francisco: Harper and Row, 1982), 122–25; and in *Border Regions of Faith: An Anthology of Religion and Social Change*, edited by Kenneth Aman (Maryknoll, NY: Orbis Books, 1987), 120–22.

———. "Should Christians Be Nuclear Pacifists?" *Towards Renewal*, Summer 1981, 13–14; and Autumn 1981, 10–11.

Reprinted in *Reaper*, August-September 1987, 11–12, 18.

1982

Kreider, Alan. "The Just Theory of War." *Strait* 5 (1982), 16–17.

Interview with James Holloway.

———. *Peacemongers*. Nottingham, Nottinghamshire, England: Shaftesbury Project, 1982.

Text and annotations for slide-tape presentation.

———. "'The Servant Is Not Greater than His Master': The Anabaptists and the Suffering Church." *Baptist Quarterly* 29 (1982): 241–66.

Reprinted in *Mennonite Quarterly Review* 58 (1984): 5–29.

———. "A Vision for Peace." *Gospel Herald*, March 30, 1982, 220–21.

1983

Kreider, Alan. "The Arms Race: The Defence Debate—Nuclear Weaponry and Pacifism." In *The Year 2000 AD*, edited by John Stott, 27–55. London: Marshall, Morgan and Scott, 1983.

———. "Christian Views on American Wars." *Fides et Historia* 16 (1983): 87–93.

———. "Shostakovich: The Man and his Music." *Third Way*, May 1983, 16–19.

Reprinted in Italian translation as "Sciostakovic, l'uome et la sua musica," *Certezze*, October-November 1983, 22–25.

———. "Swords into Ploughshares." In *Time to Choose: A Grass-Roots Study Guide on the Nuclear Arms Race from a Christian Perspective*, edited by Martha Keys Barker, et al., 54–88. Lytchett Minster, Dorset, England: Celebration Publishing, 1983.

———. *War: Christian Attitudes*. Nottingham, Nottinghamshire: Shaftesbury Project, 1983.

Reprint of annotations to *War to End All Wars* (1980).

Kreider, Eleanor. "Sister Egeria's Christmas." *Gospel Herald*, December 13, 1983, 861–62.

Reprinted in *GrassRoots*, November-December 1984, 24.

1984

Kreider, Alan. "Debate about Bomb Escalates." *GrassRoots*, January-February 1984, 4.

———. "De betekenis van de Martelaers Spiegel voor deze tijd." *Doopsgezinde Bijdragen*, n.s. 10 (1984): 11–28.

———. "God's Left Wing: The Radical Reformers." In *Heritage of Freedom*, 47–56. Tring, Hertfordshire, England: Lion Publishing, 1984.

———. "Protest and Renewal: Reformers before the Reformation." In *Heritage of Freedom*, 32–38. Tring, Hertfordshire, England: Lion Publishing, 1984.

———. "Response to Sir Frederick Catherwood." In *When Christians Disagree: Pacifism and War*, edited by Oliver Barclay,

81–84. Leicester, Leicestershire, England: Inter-Varsity Press, 1984.

———. "Too Complex for a T-Shirt: Response." *ACT Now 2* (1984), 19–20.

———, and Willard Swartley. "Pacifist Christianity: The Kingdom Way." In *When Christians Disagree: Pacifism and War,* edited by Oliver Barclay, 38–60. Leicester, Leicestershire, England: Inter-Varsity Press, 1984.

Kreider, Eleanor. "Eight is Great." *GrassRoots,* September-October 1984, 20.

———. "The Great Sunday." *Gospel Herald,* April 17, 1984, 272–73.

Reprinted in *GrassRoots,* March-April 1985, 21.

———. "The Lord's Day Is the First Day." *GrassRoots,* July-August 1984, 20.

———. "Ministers and Menus." *GrassRoots,* May-June 1984, 13.

1985

Kreider, Alan. "Colloquium Asks: What Does It Mean to Be an Anabaptist in Europe?" *Gospel Herald,* October 29, 1985, 759.

———. *God's Left Wing,* Discipleship Series 1. London: London Mennonite Centre, 1985.

Reprint of "God's Left Wing: The Radical Reformers" (1984).

———. "The Gospel No to the Bomb." In *Dropping the Bomb,* edited by John Gladwin, 74–95. London: Hodder and Stoughton, 1985.

———. "Watching or Whitewashing?" *GrassRoots,* November-December 1985, 19–21.

Reprinted in *Decide for Peace: Evangelical Christians against Nuclear Weapons,* edited by Dana Mills Powell (Basingstoke, Hampshire, England: Marshall Pickering, 1986), 62–71.

————. "Why the Christian Church Must Be Pacifist." In *Ireland and the Threat of Nuclear War*, edited by Bill McSweeney, 83–103. Dublin: Dominican Publications, 1985.

Kreider, Eleanor. "Fast and Feast." *GrassRoots*, January-February 1985, 20.

1986

Kreider, Alan. *Journey towards Holiness: A Way of Living for God's Nation*. Basingstoke, Hampshire, England: Marshall Pickering, 1986; Scottdale, PA: Herald Press, 1987.

> Received *The Other Side* Book of the Year Award, 1987; and Angel Award, Religion in Media, 1988. Condensed on cassette audiobook, narrated by Alan Kreider (Harrisonburg, VA: Choice Books, 1989). Translated into Japanese by Takio Tanase (Tokyo: Tokyo Missionary Research Institute, 2001).

————. "Participating in God's Work: How We Live Peace Church—A Testimony." In *So I Send You*. Schöffengrund, Germany: Church and Peace, 1986: 36–42.

————. "Teacher, Brother, Companion on the Way: An Appreciation of Jim Punton." *GrassRoots*, July-August 1986, 3–4.

————. "What Holiness Is." *GrassRoots*, May-June 1986, 20–21.

Kreider, Eleanor. "Miracle at the Dump." *Gospel Herald*, December 23, 1986, 874.

1987

Kreider, Alan. "Beyond Facts to Values: Debating War and Peace." *NATOWatch* 8 (June 1987), 13–16.

> Reprinted in *Wildfire* 3, no. 5 (March 1988): 32–35, 41. Published in German translation as "Richtlinien für das Gespräch mit Andersdenkenden," *Brücke (Mennonitisches Gemeindeblatt)*, November 1988, 176.

————. "The Mennonites." In *The Encyclopaedia of World Faiths*, edited by Peter Bishop and Michael Darton, 113–14. London: Macdonald Orbis, 1987.

Kreider, Eleanor. "Let the Faithful Greet Each Other: The Kiss of Peace." *Conrad Grebel Review* 5 (1987): 29–49.

1988

Kreider, Alan. "Following Jesus Implies Unconditional Pacifism." In *Handling Problems of Peace and War: An Evangelical Debate*, edited by Andrew Kirk, with John Stott and Jerram Barrs, 22–40. Basingstoke, Hampshire, England: Marshall Pickering, 1988.

———. "Our Fruits." *Free Church Chronicle* 43 (Winter 1988), 20–28.

———. "Salt and Light: 1, Preservative or Fertilizer?" *Third Way*, September 1988, 14–16.

———. "Salt and Light: 2, Table Lamp or City Lights?" *Third Way*, October 1988, 14–16.

———. "Siblings and Servants: A Mennonite View of Authority." *Christian*, May-June 1988, 22–24.

———. "Witnesses for the Defence." In *Handling Problems of Peace and War: An Evangelical Debate*, edited by Andrew Kirk, with John Stott and Jerram Barrs, 74–79. Basingstoke, Hampshire, England: Marshall Pickering, 1988.

1989

Kreider, Alan. "The Anabaptist/Mennonite Tradition." In *The Evangelicals: An Illustrated History*, edited by J. D. Allan, 24–25. Exeter, Devon, England: Paternoster Press; Grand Rapids, MI: Baker Book House, 1989.

———. "City on a Hill: Why Jesus Didn't Say, 'A Thousand Points of Light.'" *The Other Side*, May-June 1989, 34–37.
Reprint of "Salt and Light: 2, Table Lamp or City Lights?" (1988).

———. "Salty Discipleship: Bringing New Worlds to Life." *The Other Side*, March-April 1989, 34–37.

Reprint of "Salt and Light: 1, Preservative or Fertilizer?" (1988).

Kreider, Eleanor. *Enter His Gates: Fitting Worship Together.* Basingstoke, Hampshire, England: Marshall Pickering, 1989; Scottdale, PA: Herald Press, 1990.

———. "Why Do those Mennonites Do Such Funny Things?" *WMSC Voice*, April 1989, 6–8.

1990

Kreider, Alan. "England." In *The Mennonite Encyclopedia* 5, edited by Cornelius J. Dyck and Dennis D. Martin, 269–70. Scottdale, PA: Herald Press, 1990.

———. "The Growth of the Early Church: Reflections on Recent Literature." *Mission Focus* 18, no. 3 (September 1990): 33–36.

———. "London Mennonite Fellowship." In *The Mennonite Encyclopedia* 5, edited by Cornelius J. Dyck and Dennis D. Martin, 529. Scottdale, PA: Herald Press, 1990.

———. "The Relevance of Martyrs' Mirror to Our Time." *Mennonite Life* 45, no. 3 (September 1990): 9–17.

Reprint, with revisions, of "De betekenis van de Martelaers Spiegel voor deze tijd" (1984).

1991

Kreider, Alan. "Becoming a Peace Church." *Third Way*, June 1991, 19–21.

———. "Be Yourself When You Pray!" *Alpha*, September 1991, 18–20.

Interview with John Buckeridge.

———. "Holiness." *Guidelines to the Bible* (Bible Reading Fellowship), January-April 1991, 9–30.
Three weeks of Bible studies.

———. "Peacemaking: The Laboratory of God's Future." *Wildfire* 6, no. 1 (Winter 1991): 26–29, 50.

Kreider, Eleanor. "Which Bible Version?" *Double Image [Men, Women and God]*, Autumn 1991, 6–7.

1992

Kreider, Alan. "The Search for Roots." *Anabaptism Today* 1 (November 1992): 5–11.

Kreider, Eleanor. "Does It Matter Which Bible Translation We Use?" *Gospel Herald*, June 16, 1992, 6–8.
Reprint of "Which Bible Version?" (1991).

———. "Love Is the Measure." *Goshen College Bulletin*, March 1992, 3.

1993

Kreider, Alan. "Abolishing the Laity: An Anabaptist Perspective on Ordination." In *Anyone for Ordination?* edited by Paul Beasley-Murray, 84–111. Tunbridge Wells, Kent, England: Monarch, 1993.

———. "The Anabaptist Heritage." *Faith and Freedom* 2, no. 2 (June 1993), 9–12.
Reprint of "The Search for Roots" (1992).

———. Foreword to *The Community of the Spirit: How the Church Is in the World*, by C. Norman Kraus, 6–8. Scottdale, PA: Herald Press, 1993.

———. Foreword to *Kingdom Come*, by Christopher D. Marshall, 9–10. Auckland, NZ: Impetus, 1993.

———. "God's Grace Is Not for Hoarding." *Gospel Herald*, June 22, 1993, 1–3.

Kreider, Eleanor. "The Lord's Supper." *Anabaptism Today* 2 (February 1993): 8–17.

———. "Snapshots of Kingdom People." *Anabaptism Today* 4 (October 1993): 2–3.

1994

Kreider, Alan. "An Anabaptist Looks at the Past." *Anabaptism Today* 4 (February 1994): 3–6.

>   Abridged from "Mennonite/Anabaptist Perceptions of Relationships with the Church of England" (1994).

———. "Mennonite/Anabaptist Perceptions of Relationships with the Church of England." *Crucible*, January-March 1994, 3–18.

———. "Worship and Evangelism in Pre-Christendom (The Laing Lecture 1994)." *Vox Evangelica* 24 (1994): 7–38.

Kreider, Eleanor. "A Two-Edged Sword?" *Alpha*, July 1994, 21–23.

>   Reprint of "Which Bible Version?" (1991).

———. "A Vision of Multi-Voiced Worship: Involving the Whole People." *Anabaptism Today* 5 (February 1994): 13–17.

1995

Kreider, Alan. "Lessons from Intentional Communities: Mennonite Perspectives." *Theology Themes*, Autumn 1995, 18–24.

———. "Mennonite Ethics." In *New Dictionary of Christian Ethics and Pastoral Theology*, edited by David J. Atkinson, 584–85. Leicester, Leicestershire, England: Inter-Varsity Press, 1995.

———. "Menno Simons." In *New Dictionary of Christian Ethics and Pastoral Theology*, edited by David J. Atkinson, 585. Leicester, Leicestershire, England: Inter-Varsity Press, 1995.

————. "Training the Reflexes: Recovering Anabaptist Spirituality." *Anabaptism Today* 10 (October 1995): 12–17.

————. *Worship and Evangelism in Pre-Christendom*. Alcuin/ GROW Joint Liturgical Studies 32. Cambridge, England: Grove Books, 1995.

> Expanded from "Worship and Evangelism in Pre-Christendom (The Laing Lecture 1994)," *Vox Evangelica* 24 (1994): 7–38. Published in Korean translation (Seoul: Korea Anabaptist Center, 2003).

Kreider, Eleanor. "Jesus Bowls a Googly." *Gospel Herald*, May 16, 1995, 6–7.

1996

Kreider, Alan. "Baptism, Catechism, and the Eclipse of Jesus' Teaching in Early Christianity." *Tyndale Bulletin* 47 (1996): 315–48.

> Reprinted in *Mennonite Quarterly Review* 72 (1998): 5–30.

————. "Disciplines of Community—Some Mennonite Perspectives." *Christian Community* 73 (Spring 1996), 3–5.

> Abridged from "Lessons from Intentional Communities: Mennonite Perspectives" (1995).

————. "God's Grace Is Sufficient for Me." In *Godward: Personal Stories of Grace*, edited by Ted Koontz, 74–84. Scottdale, PA: Herald Press, 1996.

Kreider, Eleanor. "The Church as a Community in Worship." *Anabaptism Today* 13 (October 1996): 3–7.

1997

Kreider, Alan. "Christ, Culture and Truth-Telling." *Conrad Grebel Review* 15 (Fall 1997): 207–33.

> Reprinted in *Faith in the Centre: Christianity and Culture*, edited by Paul S. Fiddes (Macon, GA: Smyth and Helwys, 2001), 27–60.

Kreider, Eleanor. "Alive to the Spirit." In *Alive to God: Bible Guidelines for Living by the Spirit*, July-September. Milton Keynes, Buckinghamshire, England: Scripture Union, 1997, 38–43, 58–61, 74–82.

———. *Communion Shapes Character*. Scottdale, PA: Herald Press, 1997.

1998

Kreider, Alan. Foreword to *A Believing Church*, by Keith G. Jones, xiii–xv. Didcot, Oxfordshire, England: Baptist Union, 1998.

———. Foreword to *The Great Restoration: The Religious Radicals of the 16th and 17th Centuries*, by Meic Pearse, ix–xi. Carlisle, Cumbria, England: Paternoster Press, 1998.

———. "Is a Peace Church Possible?" *Anabaptism Today* 19 (Autumn 1998): 4–16.

———. "Early Christian Writings, with Commentary." *MERC Izumi* 17 (1998).

Published in Japanese translation.

Kreider, Eleanor. *Given for You: A Fresh Look at Communion*. Leicester, Leicestershire, England: Inter-Varsity Press, 1998.

Reprint of *Communion Shapes Character* (1997).

———. "Praying for Peace." *Anabaptism Today* 17 (Spring 1998): 3–7.

———. "Worship: True to Jesus." In *Music in Worship: A Mennonite Perspective*, edited by Bernie Neufeld, 3–30. Scottdale, PA: Herald Press, 1998.

Abridged in *Anabaptism Today* 34 (October 2003): 3–12.

1999

Kreider, Alan. *The Change of Conversion and the Origin of Christendom.* Harrisburg, PA: Trinity Press International, 1999. Reprinted (Eugene, OR: Wipf and Stock, 2007).

———. "Conversion." In *Encyclopedia of Early Christianity*, 2nd ed., edited by Everett Ferguson, 1:288–89. New York: Garland Publishing, 1999.

———. "Is a Peace Church Possible? The Church's 'Domestic' Life." *Anabaptism Today* 20 (Spring 1999): 3–13.

———. "Is a Peace Church Possible? The Church's 'Foreign Policy'—Work, War, Witness." *Anabaptism Today* 22 (Autumn 1999): 3–13.

———. "Is a Peace Church Possible? The Church's 'Foreign Policy'—Worship." *Anabaptism Today* 21 (Summer 1999): 3–11.

———. "Oaths." In *Encyclopedia of Early Christianity*, 2nd ed., edited by Everett Ferguson, 2:823–24. New York: Garland Publishing, 1999.

———. *Peace Church, Mission Church: Friends or Foes?* Mission Insight 6. Elkhart, IN: Mennonite Board of Missions, 1999.

———, and Jane Shaw, editors. *Culture and the Nonconformist Tradition.* Cardiff: University of Wales Press, 1999.

Kreider, Eleanor. "Anabaptist Spirituality: Learning to Pray the Prisoners' Way." *The Way* 39, no. 3 (1999): 281–92.

2000

Kreider, Alan. Foreword to *Beyond Tithing*, by Stuart Murray, xi–xiii. Carlisle, Cumbria, England: Paternoster, 2000.

———. "Response to Oliver O'Donovan's 'Mission, Coercion and Christendom.'" *The Gospel and Our Culture* 27 (Spring 2000): 5.

————. "When Anabaptists Were Last in the British Isles." In *Coming Home: Stories of Anabaptists in Britain and Ireland,* edited by Alan Kreider and Stuart Murray, 176–92. Kitchener, ON: Pandora Press, 2000.

> Reprint of "Mennonite/Anabaptist Perceptions of Relationships with the Church of England" (1994).

————, and Eleanor Kreider. *Becoming a Peace Church.* London: New Ground, 2000.

> Published in Korean translation (Seoul: Korea Anabaptist Center, 2003).

————, and Eleanor Kreider. "Enabling the Anabaptist Voice to Sing (interview with Stuart Murray)." *Anabaptism Today* 24 (2000): 4–11.

————, and Stuart Murray, editors. *Coming Home: Stories of Anabaptists in Britain and Ireland.* Kitchener, ON: Pandora Press, 2000.

Kreider, Eleanor. "The Disciple Is Not above the Master: Anabaptist Spirituality." *Anabaptism Today* 23 (Spring 2000): 10–19.

> Abridged from "Anabaptist Spirituality: Learning to Pray the Prisoners' Way" (1999).

2001

Kreider, Alan. *Anabaptist Christianity: Revived and Relevant.* Mission Insight 16. Elkhart, IN: Mennonite Board of Missions, 2001.

————, "Changing Patterns of Conversion in the West." In *The Origins of Christendom in the West,* edited by Alan Kreider, 3–46. Edinburgh: T & T Clark, 2001.

————, editor. *The Origins of Christendom in the West.* Edinburgh: T & T Clark, 2001.

————. "Then One Day I Lost the Bible." *Christian Living,* October-November 2001, 19–20.

————, and Donald Hay, editors. *Christianity and the Culture of Economics.* Cardiff: University of Wales Press, 2001.

————, and Eleanor Kreider. "Economical with the Truth: Swearing and Lying—An Anabaptist Perspective." *Brethren in Christ History and Life* 24 (2001): 152–77.

2002

Kreider, Alan. "Conversion and Culture in Early Christianity." *Journal of Hokkaido Bunkyo University* 3 (2002): 49–67.

Reprinted in *Journal of the Academy for Evangelism in Theological Education* 19 (2003–2004): 12–29.

————. "Initiation: Becoming Resident Aliens." *Mennonite Life* 57, no. 2 (June 2002).

————. "Letter from America." *Anabaptism Today* 29 (2002): 3–8.

————. "The Two Edges of Confession." *Vision: A Journal for Church and Theology* 3, no. 2 (Fall 2002): 36–43.

Reprinted in *Canadian Mennonite*, June 2, 2003, 6–9.

2003

Kreider, Alan. "Beyond Bosch: The Early Church and the Christendom Shift." *Mission Focus* 11, Supplement (2003): 158–77.

Reprinted in *International Bulletin for Missionary Research* 29, no. 2 (2005): 59–68; and in *Speaking about What We Have Seen and Heard: Evangelism in Global Perspective*, edited by Jonathan J. Bonk, Dwight P. Baker, Daniel J. Nicholas, and Craig A. Noll (New Haven, CT: OMSC Publications, 2007), 13–36.

————. "Military Service in the Church Orders." *Journal of Religious Ethics* 31, no. 3 (2003): 415–42.

————. "Tribute to Ben Faulkner." *Anabaptism Today* 33 (June 2003): 26–27.

————, and Stephen Darlington, editors. *Composing Music for Worship.* Norwich: Canterbury Press, 2003.

2004

Kreider, Alan. "Apprentices in Faith: Ten Proposals for Our Day, Inspired by Ancient Baptism Practices." *Leader*, Summer 2004, 2–5.

————. "'Not Only a Borrower but a Lender Be': Mennonite Piety in Dialogue with Charismatic Christianity." *DreamSeeker Magazine* 4, no. 4 (Autumn 2004): 17–22.

————. "Peacemaking in Worship in the Syrian Church Orders." *Studia Liturgica* 34, no. 2 (2004): 177–90.

————. "A Post Dialogue-Conversation." In *On Baptism: Mennonite-Catholic Theological Colloquium, 2001–2002*, Bridgefolk Series, edited by Gerald W. Schlabach, 112–17, 128–38, 142–46. Kitchener, ON: Pandora Press, 2004.

————. "A Post-Dialogue Conversation II." In *On Baptism: Mennonite-Catholic Theological Colloquium, 2001–2002*, Bridgefolk Series, edited by Gerald W. Schlabach, 112–17, 128–38, 142–46. Kitchener, ON: Pandora Press, 2004.

————. "Response." In *On Baptism: Mennonite-Catholic Theological Colloquium, 2001–2002*, Bridgefolk Series, edited by Gerald W. Schlabach, 80–86. Kitchener, ON: Pandora Press, 2004.

Kreider, Eleanor. *Introduction to the Theology and Practice of Christian Worship.* Distance Learning Degree in Theology, Level 3 BA (Hons), The Open Theological College. Cheltenham, Gloucestershire, England: University of Gloucestershire, 2004.

2005

Kreider, Alan. "Masculine Spirituality: Four Crucial Areas for Being a Christian Male." *The Mennonite*, September 20, 2005, 8–10.

————. "Missiologist Honored by Colleagues at AMBS." *Mennonite Weekly Review*, December 12, 2005, 8.

————, Eleanor Kreider, and Paulus Widjaja. *A Culture of Peace: God's Vision for the Church*. Intercourse, PA: Good Books, 2005.

Published in German translation as *Eine Kultur des Friedens: Gottes Vision für Gemeinde und Welt* (Schwarzenfeld, Germany: Neufeld Verlag, 2008).

Kreider, Eleanor. "Creating a Daily Office for Mennonites." *Vision: A Journal for Church and Theology* 6, no. 1 (Spring 2005): 77–83.

2006

Kreider, Alan. "Anabaptist/Mennonite Identity." *MERC Izumi* 21 (2006).

Published in Japanese translation.

————. "Closets and Worries." *RAD Newsletter* 2, no. 4 (Summer 2006), 1, 3.

————. "Holiness and Risk (Acts 10)." *MERC Izumi* 21 (2006).

Published in Japanese translation.

————. "The Recovery of Witness." *The Mennonite*, November 7, 2006, 8–10.

Reprinted in *Our Faith* (Spring 2007): 12–13.

————. "West Europe in Missional Perspective: Themes from Mennonite Mission, 1950–2004." In *Evangelical, Ecumenical, and Anabaptist Missiologies in Conversation: Essays in Honor of Wilbert R. Shenk*, edited by James R. Krabill, Walter Sawatsky, and Charles E. Van Engen, 206–15. Maryknoll, NY: Orbis Books, 2006.

2007

Boers, Arthur Paul, Barbara Nelson Gingerich, Eleanor Kreider, John Rempel, and Mary H. Schertz, editors. *Take Our
Moments and Our Days: An Anabaptist Prayer Book.* Vol. 1: *Ordinary Time.* Scottdale PA: Herald Press, 2007.

Kreider, Alan. "Ancient Church." In *Encyclopedia of Mission and
Missionaries,* edited by Jonathan J. Bonk, 13–14. New York and
London: Routledge, 2007.

———. "Baptism and Catechesis as Spiritual Formation." In
Remembering Our Future: Explorations in Deep Church, edited
by Andrew Walker and Luke Bretherton, 170–206. Milton
Keynes, Buckinghamshire, England: Paternoster Press, 2007.

———. "Beauty of Life Causes Strangers to Join." *Cell-UK Magazine* 326 (2007), 6.

———. "Christendom." In *Encyclopedia of Mission and Missionaries,* edited by Jonathan J. Bonk, 73–78. New York and London:
Routledge, 2007.

———. "Rome." In *The Way Is Made by Walking,* by Arthur Paul
Boers, 202–3. Downers Grove, IL: IVP Books, 2007.

———. "Violence and Mission in the Fourth and Fifth Centuries,
with Lessons for Today." *International Bulletin of Missionary
Research* 31, no. 3 (2007): 125–33.

2008

Kreider, Alan. *Social Holiness: A Way of Living for God's Nation.*
Eugene, OR: Wipf and Stock, 2008.

Reprint of *Journey towards Holiness A Way of Living for God's Nation*
(1986). Afterword by Dale M. Coulter.

———. "'They Alone Know the Right Way to Live': The Early
Church and Evangelism." In *Ancient Faith for the Church's*

Future, edited by Mark Husbands and Jeffrey P. Greenman, 169–86. Downers Grove, IL: InterVarsity Press, 2008.

———. *Tongue Screws and Testimony.* Missio Dei 16. Elkhart, IN: Mennonite Mission Network, 2008.

———, and Eleanor Kreider. "Dirk Willems and Discipleship." *Reunion: The Menno-Hof Newsletter* 17, no. 3 (Spring 2008), 1–2.

2009

Kreider, Alan. *Resident but Alien: How the Early Church Grew.* Harpenden, Hertfordshire, England: Great Commission Distribution Ltd. (YWAM), 2009.

Six half-hour presentations on two DVDs.

———, and Eleanor Kreider. *Worship and Mission after Christendom.* Milton Keynes, Buckinghamshire, England: Paternoster Press, 2009; Scottdale, PA: Herald Press, 2011.

Kreider, Eleanor. "Communion Questions: Communion and Mission Can Go Together." *The Mennonite,* February 17, 2009, 16–17.

2010

Boers, Arthur Paul, Barbara Nelson Gingerich, Eleanor Kreider, John Rempel, and Mary H. Schertz, editors. *Take Our Moments and Our Days: An Anabaptist Prayer Book.* Vol. 2: *Advent through Pentecost.* Scottdale PA: Herald Press, 2010.

Kreider, Alan. "Learning to Live Like Christians: On the Peace Witness of the Early Church." *The Sign of Peace: Journal of the Catholic Peace Fellowship* 9, no. 1 (Spring 2010): 21–24.

2011

Kreider, Alan. "Conversion." In *The Cambridge Dictionary of Christian Theology,* edited by Ian A. McFarland, David A. S.

Fergusson, Karen Kilby, and Iain R. Torrence, 115–16. Cambridge: Cambridge University Press, 2011.

———. "From Mennonite to Anabaptist: Mennonite Witness in England since 1974." In *History and Mission in Europe: Continuing the Conversation*, edited by Mary Raber and Peter F. Penner, 237–60. Schwarzenfeld, Germany: Neufeld Verlag, 2011.

———. "Revisioning Identity: Mennonite Reflections on Narrative." In *Questions of Identity: Studies in Honour of Brian Haymes*, edited by Anthony R. Cross and Ruth Gouldbourne, 207–38. Oxford: Regent's Park College, 2011.

Contributors

Laura Lehman Amstutz is the communication coordinator for Eastern Mennonite Seminary. She is part of the leadership team at The Table, a worshiping community in Harrisonburg, Virginia.

Simon Barrow is a writer, independent theologian, and co-director of the Anabaptist-influenced Christian think tank Ekklesia. He was formerly assistant general secretary and global mission secretary of Churches Together in Britain and Ireland, the official ecumenical body.

Janie and Neal Blough have served in France with Mennonite Mission Network for more than thirty-five years. During that time they have also been active in the lives of two urban multicultural congregations. At present they are involved in the ministry of the Paris Mennonite Center.

Jonathan Bonk is one of North America's prominent missiologists. He serves as director of the Overseas Ministries Study Center, New Haven, Connecticut; and as editor of the *International Bulletin of Missionary Research*.

Shana Peachey Boshart is conference youth minister for Central Plains Mennonite Conference of Mennonite Church USA. She lives in rural Parnell, Iowa.

Erin Dufault-Hunter is assistant professor of Christian Ethics in the School of Theology at Fuller Theological Seminary, Pasadena, California. Her current research focuses on sexuality and bioethics in the twenty-first century. She is a long-time member of Pasadena Mennonite Church, where she helps lead worship and occasionally preaches.

Tim Foley became a Mennonite pastor in London before moving to Northern Ireland to work with an Anabaptist congregation and in mediation. He now works as the director for Europe program at the Mennonite Mission Network.

Anna Geyer is a wife and mother in rural Iowa. She farms with her husband, raises flowers for cutting, and bakes bread and pizza in a masonry oven for farmers markets and community gatherings.

Brian Haymes is a Baptist minister and former principal of Northern Baptist College, Manchester, England, and Bristol Baptist College. He is also a member of the Anabaptist Network theology forum and author of several books on Baptist identity and theology.

H. Eugene Herr has served in many phases of discipleship ministries in the Mennonite Church. From 1985 to 2001 he and his wife, Mary, created and directed The Hermitage, a place of retreat and spiritual formation near Three Rivers, Michigan.

Michele Hershberger is chair of the Bible and Ministry Division at Hesston College, in Hesston, Kansas. Author of *A Christian View of Hospitality*, she enjoys preaching and writing on the topic of hospitality.

Catherine Horton is a schoolteacher working with four- and five-year-olds in a multicultural inner city primary school in Wolverhampton, England. She is married to Chris, and they have three grown-up children. Together with Chris she is involved in a city center church and in a neighborhood "fresh expression" of church in west Wolverhampton.

Moriah Hurst works in Melbourne, Australia, with Mennonite Mission Network, for Praxis, training Christian practitioners of youth work. She also teaches in an inner city ministry called Urban Seed. She studied under Alan Kreider at Associated Mennonite Biblical Seminary in Elkhart, Indiana, and is still grappling with some of the questions raised in his classes.

Andy Brubacher Kaethler is instructor of Faith Formation and Culture at Associated Mennonite Biblical Seminary in Elkhart, Indiana. He was previously a youth minister in Ontario, Canada.

Juliet Kilpin is a Baptist minister. She was co-leader of the first Urban Expression church planting team in London, and is now one of the coordinators of this developing urban mission agency.

Kyong-Jung Kim, director of the Korea Anabaptist Center, grew up in South Korea. He studied physics in Korea and theology at the Canadian Mennonite Bible College in Winnipeg, Manitoba. He has been serving at KAC since 2001, living in Chuncheon, Korea, with his wife, Ellen, and two daughters, Grace and Sophia.

James R. Krabill has served with Mennonite mission agencies since 1976 in West Africa, England, France, and the United States. From 1978 to 1988 he taught Bible and church history with Mennonite Board of Missions among African-initiated movements, mostly the Harrist Church, in Ivory Coast, West Africa. Since 2002, he has served as senior executive for the Global Ministries division of Mennonite Mission Network.

Matthew Krabill lives in Pasadena, California, where he has completed MA degrees in Theology and Intercultural Studies at Fuller Theological Seminary. He is enrolled in PhD studies at Fuller to explore the impact of immigrant congregations on Mennonite Church USA.

J. Nelson Kraybill is lead pastor at Prairie Street Mennonite Church, Elkhart, Indiana. In recent years he has served as president of Associated Mennonite Biblical Seminary, Elkhart (1997–2009); programme director of London Mennonite Centre (1991–96); and author of *Apocalypse and Allegiance: Worship, Politics, and Devotion in the Book of Revelation* (Brazos Press, 2010).

Andrew Kreider is the son of Alan and Eleanor Kreider. He was born and raised in London, read theology at Cambridge University, and trained for the ministry at Associated Mennonite Biblical

Seminary, Elkhart, Indiana. For eleven years he served as pastor of Prairie Street Mennonite Church, Elkhart. Kreider is a musician and poet. He is married to Katie, and they have three children and live in Elkhart.

Joseph Liechty worked for Mennonite Board of Missions in Ireland and Northern Ireland, 1980–2003. Since 2003 he has been professor of Peace, Justice, and Conflict Studies at Goshen College in Goshen, Indiana, and serves as editor of the *Journal of Religion, Conflict and Peace* (www.religionconflictpeace.org).

Jim Longley works as a bank executive, having previously been chief executive of Anglican Retirement Villages (1996–2000), a member of Parliament in New South Wales (1986–96), and government minister for Community Services, Aboriginal Affairs, and Aging (1992–95).

Sally Longley is working part-time as a spiritual director and retreat leader with the Canisius Centre for Ignatian Spirituality in Sydney, Australia, and part-time as an honorary associate minister with an Anglican parish.

Chris Marshall teaches in the Religious Studies Department, Victoria University, Wellington, New Zealand. He is a New Testament scholar who is a world authority on restorative justice. He has authored several books, including *Beyond Retribution: A New Testament Vision for Justice, Crime and Punishment* (Grand Rapids, MI: Eerdmans, 2001).

Glen Marshall is a Baptist minister and a tutor with Northern Baptist Learning Community in Manchester, England. His interests include mission, preaching, and contemporary evangelicalism. He is involved in a number of local pioneering mission initiatives, including Urban Expression and Ellesmere Port Community Ministry.

Cyneatha Millsaps is lead pastor of Community Mennonite Church in Markham, Illinois. She is a community activist and advocate for the needs of women and children in the areas of violence, education, and spiritual development.

Lesley Misrahi first met Alan and Ellie Kreider at the London Mennonite Centre, and it was their ministry that drew her to Wood Green Mennonite Church, of which she was a member for many years, until her death in May 2011. Her background was in health and social care policy, and she was a lay member of the Mental Health Review Tribunal.

Noel Moules founded the Workshop Christian learning program, which he has directed since 1983. He is a committed peace, justice, and creation spirituality activist; a trustee of the Anabaptist Network; and a popular teacher, speaker, and writer.

Sian Murray Williams is a Baptist minister and the moderator of the Baptist Union of Great Britain's Faith and Unity Executive. She was formerly director for missionaries at BMS World Mission and currently serves as a tutor for worship studies at Bristol Baptist College.

Stuart Murray Williams works as a trainer and consultant under the auspices of the Anabaptist Network. Based in Bristol, England, he travels widely in the UK and overseas and works with local churches, mission agencies, denominational leaders, conferences, and individuals. His particular areas of expertise are in church planting, emerging church, urban mission, mission in post-Christendom, and Anabaptist history and theology.

David Nussbaum has, since 2007, been chief executive of the environmental charity WWF-UK and a non-executive director of Low Carbon Accelerator and of Shared Interest. He has wide executive and non-executive experience in public companies and international charities (Transparency International, Oxfam, Traidcraft plc) and serves as a trustee of the Anabaptist Network. Nussbaum has two degrees in theology and one in finance.

Cathy Nobles is originally from the USA and lived in Switzerland and throughout the Middle East before moving to the UK. She works with Youth with a Mission, continuing the training work begun on the Reconciliation Walk.

Lloyd Pietersen is a New Testament scholar with PhD from the University of Sheffield; director of Advanced Workshop; trustee of the Anabaptist Network; lecturer at the University of Gloucestershire; and author of *The Polemic of the Pastorals: A Sociological Examination of the Development of Pauline Christianity* (Sheffield Academic Press, 2004); and *Reading the Bible after Christendom* (Paternoster, 2011).

Janet Plenert has an MA in theological studies in Mission and Church Leadership from Associated Mennonite Biblical Seminary, Elkhart, Indiana, and is passionate about the church as God's strategy for redeeming the world. She is a former mission worker in Congo and Brazil, and until recently served as executive secretary of Mennonite Church Canada Witness. She is vice president of Mennonite World Conference.

John Rempel is a Mennonite minister and professor of Historical Theology and Anabaptist Studies at Associated Mennonite Biblical Seminary in Elkhart, Indiana. He speaks and writes on historical, theological, and liturgical subjects.

Tony Richie is an ordained bishop in the Church of God (Cleveland, Tennessee) and chair of the Church of God/Mennonite Church USA dialogue. He is a pastor, theologian, teacher, and writer, with a PhD from London School of Theology. He represents Pentecostals with the World Council of Churches and is the author of *Speaking by the Spirit: A Pentecostal Model for Interreligious Encounter & Dialogue* (Emeth, 2010).

Ian Stackhouse has a PhD from London School of Theology and currently serves as pastoral leader of Guildford Baptist Church. He is the author of several books and articles, including *The Gospel-*

Driven Church (Paternoster, 2004), and *The Day is Yours: Slow Spirituality in a Fast-Moving World* (Paternoster, 2008).

Kim Tan is chairman of Spring Hill Management Ltd, a specialist life sciences and social venture capital investment company. He is also an advisor to a number of government agencies in Asia on biotechnology, a Fellow of the Royal Society of Medicine, and cofounder of the Transformational Business Network. His most recent book is *The Jubilee Gospel* (Authentic, 2008).

Marty Troyer loves living in Houston, Texas, with his wife, Hannah; son, Malakai; daughter, Clara; and excitable dog, Chubs. He is the pastor of Houston Mennonite Church, and blogs weekly for the *Houston Chronicle* as *The Peace Pastor* at http://blog.chron.com/thepeacepastor/.

Mark Van Steenwyk is a founding member of Missio Dei, an Anabaptist intentional community in Minneapolis, Minnesota. He is a grassroots educator and networker for emerging radical communities and the general editor of JesusRadicals.com.

Paulus Widjaja teaches at Duta Wacana Christian University in Jogjakarta, Indonesia. He is a Mennonite pastor and current president of the United Muria Christian Churches of Indonesia, one of the three Mennonite conferences in Indonesia. Widjaja also serves as Mennonite World Conference Peace Commission secretary. The book he co-wrote with Alan and Eleanor Kreider, *A Culture of Peace: God's Vision for the Church*, was the 2005 selection for the MWC Global Anabaptist-Mennonite Shelf of Literature.

Anne Wilkinson-Hayes is a Baptist regional minister in Melbourne, Australia, and the former social action adviser for the Baptist Union of Great Britain.

Sean Winter is a Baptist minister and a published author. He was formerly tutor in New Testament at Northern Baptist College, Manchester, and is currently professor of New Testament at the Uniting Church Theological College in Melbourne, Australia.

Sally Schreiner Youngquist is community leader of Reba Place Fellowship, a Christian intentional community in Evanston and Chicago, Illinois. She was a founding pastor of Living Water Community Church and served on the board of directors for Mennonite Board of Missions from 1991 to 2001.

Veronica Zundel is a freelance writer living in North London, who has been a member of Wood Green Mennonite Church for nearly two decades. Her books include *The Time of our Lives,* and *Crying for the Light,* an exploration of depression through Bible reading notes, reflections and poems (both published by Bible Reading Fellowship; *Crying* also published by Kregel in the US). Her book *Everything I Know about God, I've Learned from Being a Parent* will be published by BRF in 2013. She is married and has a teenage son with Asperger Syndrome.

9 780836 196023